AA

D0308094

50 Walks in

WILTSHIRE

This book is to be returned on or before
the last date stamped below.

First published 2002
Researched and written by David Hancock

Produced by AA Publishing
© Automobile Association Developments Limited 2002
Illustrations © Automobile Association Developments Limited 2002
Reprinted 2004 (twice), 2005 (twice)

Published by AA Publishing (a trading name of Automobile Association
Developments Limited, whose registered office is from is Fanum House, Basing
View, Basingstoke, Hampshire, RG21 4EA;
registered number 1878835).

OS Ordnance Survey® This product includes mapping data licensed from
Ordnance Survey® with the permission of the Controller
of Her Majesty's Stationery Office.
© Crown copyright 2005. All rights reserved. Licence number 399221

ISBN-10: 0 7495-3335-8
ISBN-13: 978-0-7495-3335-9

A CIP catalogue record for this book is available
from the British Library.

The contents of this book are believed correct at the time of printing.
Nevertheless, the publishers cannot be held responsible for any errors or
omissions or for changes in the details given in this book or for the
consequences of any reliance on the information it provides. This does not
affect your statutory rights. We have tried to ensure accuracy in this book, but
things do change and we would be grateful if readers would advise us of any
inaccuracies they may encounter.

We have taken all reasonable steps to ensure that these walks are safe and
achievable by walkers with a realistic level of fitness. However, all outdoor
activities involve a degree of risk and the publishers accept no responsibility
for any injuries caused to readers whilst following these walks. For more advice
on walking safely see page 128. The mileage range shown on the front cover is
for guidance only – some walks may exceed or be less than these distances.

Visit the AA Publishing website at www.theAA.com/bookshop

Paste-up and editorial by Outcrop Publishing Services Ltd, Cumbria,
for AA Publishing

A02859

Printed in Italy by G Canale & C SPA, Torino, Italy

Legend

←-------	Walk route	P	Car park
••••••	Optional walk route	~~~	Cliff
-------	Adjoining footpath		Rock outcrop
—·—·—	County boundary		Beach
☼	Viewpoint	♠ ♣	Woodland
▲ 392	Spot height		Parkland
	Built-up area	†	Church, cathedral, chapel
●	Place of interest	WC	Toilet
△	Steep section	⊼	Picnic area

Wiltshire locator map

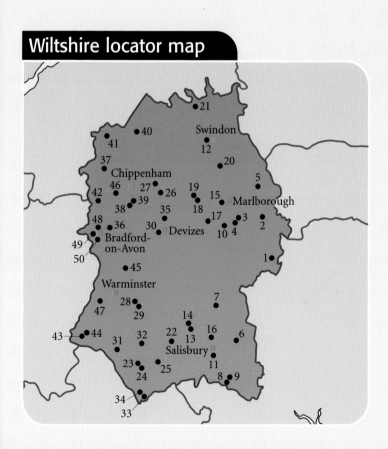

Contents

Contents

Rating: Each walk is rated for its relative difficulty compared to the other walks in this book. Walks marked 🚶 🚶 🚶 are likely to be shorter and easier with little total ascent. The hardest walks are marked 🚶🚶 🚶🚶 🚶🚶 .

Walking in Safety: For advice and safety tips ➤ 128.

Introducing Wiltshire

A land shrouded in mystery, myth and legend, Wiltshire evokes images of ancient stone circles, white chalk horses carved into hillsides, crop circles and the forbidden, empty landscape of Salisbury Plain. To many M4 and A303 travellers heading west out of London through the clutter of the Thames Valley, Wiltshire is where the landscape opens out and rural England begins.

Wiltshire's charm lies in the beauty of its countryside. The expansive chalk landscapes of the Marlborough and Pewsey downs and Cranborne Chase inspire a sense of space and freedom, offering miles of uninterrupted views deep into Dorset, Somerset and the Cotswolds. South Wiltshire is characterised by the crystal waters of the Ebble, Avon, Nadder and Wylye rivers meandering through tranquil valleys etched into the chalk, linking picture-postcard villages, on their way to Salisbury and its majestic cathedral. Jurassic limestone forms the county's north west border. This is the south east edge of the Cotswolds,

characterised by its gently undulating landscape and the distinctive, honey-coloured stone buildings of Castle Combe, Bradford-on-Avon, Malmesbury and Corsham.

Although famous the world over for the prehistoric sites of Avebury and Stonehenge, Wiltshire has much more to offer the walker who is keen to explore the 2,500 miles (4,022km) of public footpaths that criss-cross the county. Several long distance trails pass through Wiltshire, including the Ridgeway, the Thames Path and the Macmillan Way. The circular White Horse Trail visits all Wiltshire's white chalk horses in its 90 miles (145km), and the 30 mile (48km), circular Imber Range Perimeter Path circumnavigates the army's training area on Salisbury Plain.

Understandably, many of the routes described in this book traverse sweeping chalk downlands in search of ancient paths, barrows, monoliths and hill forts, and the best views. You can stride across the sarsen-strewn landscape of Fyfield Down near Marlborough, walk in the footsteps of Civil War soldiers on Roundway Down above Devizes, and locate two of Wiltshire's famous White Horses on Milk Hill and Westbury Hill. Some walks combine invigorating hilltops with tranquil valleys and riverside strolls or tow path walking beside the Kennet and Avon Canal.

Wiltshire's thriving markets towns and picturesque villages provide interesting starting points and welcome diversions along the way. Stroll through quaint timbered and

---

PUBLIC TRANSPORT ⓘ

Wiltshire's good network of bus and rail services provides a convenient way of accessing the county's market towns, villages and tourist attractions. Walks 2, 10, 11, 46, 48/49 and 50 start close to railway stations. For train times call the 24-hour national train information line on 08457 48 49 50. For details of the wide range of public transport services across the county, call the Wiltshire Traveline 08457 09 08 99. You can also get travel information from the national public transport enquiry line on 0870 608 2608 or look on the internet at www.pti.org.uk.

thatched villages in the southern Woodford and Avon valleys and explore the historic streets of the stone villages of Lacock, Castle Combe and Sherston. Walk around Salisbury and discover architectural styles from the 13th century to the present and take time to visit the city's elegant cathedral and fascinating museums. At Devizes, trace the medieval street pattern and admire some grand buildings before following the Kennet and Avon Canal tow path to the famous Caen Hill flight of 29 locks, one of the great wonders of the canal era.

Wiltshire is richly endowed with manor houses, stately mansions and beautiful gardens. With this collection of walks, you can stroll past Bowood House, Longleat House, Lacock Abbey and Corsham Court, and enjoy a walk between The Courts at Holt and Great Chalfield Manor. Among the impressive gardens, Stourhead stands out, as one of England's finest 18th-century landscaped gardens.

This guide should help you to discover that Wiltshire offers some of the best walking to be found anywhere in lowland, rural England.

Using this Book

Information panels

An information panel for each walk shows its relative difficulty (➤ 5), the distance and total amount of ascent. An indication of the gradients you will encounter is shown by the rating 🔺🔺🔺 (no steep slopes) to 🔺🔺🔺 (several very steep slopes).

Maps

There are 30 maps, covering 40 of the walks. Some walks have a suggested option in the same area. The information panel for these walks will tell you how much extra walking is involved. On short-cut suggestions the panel will tell you the total distance if you set out from the start of the main walk. Where an option returns to the same point on the main walk, just the distance of the loop is given. Where an option leaves the main walk at one point and returns to it at another, then the distance shown is for the whole walk. The minimum time suggested is for reasonably fit walkers and doesn't allow for stops. Each walk has a suggested map. Laminated aqua3 maps are longer lasting and water resistant.

Start Points

The start of each walk is given as a six-figure grid reference prefixed by two letters indicating which 100km square of the National Grid it refers to. You'll find more information on grid references on most Ordnance Survey maps.

Dogs

We have tried to give dog owners useful advice about how dog friendly each walk is. Please respect other countryside users. Keep your dog under control, especially around livestock, and obey local bylaws and other dog control notices.

Car Parking

Many of the car parks suggested are public, but occasionally you may find you have to park on the roadside or in a lay-by. Please be considerate when you leave your car, ensuring that access roads or gates are not blocked and that other vehicles can pass safely.

Walk 1

Border Paths Around the Chutes

Explore the hills and combes close to the Wiltshire/Hampshire border.

•DISTANCE•	8 miles (12.9km)
•MINIMUM TIME•	4hrs 15min
•ASCENT / GRADIENT•	1,099ft (335m) ▲▲▲
•LEVEL OF DIFFICULTY•	👫 👫 👫
•PATHS•	Bridle paths, downland tracks, field paths, roads, 8 stiles
•LANDSCAPE•	Farmland, woodland, downland pasture, village streets
•SUGGESTED MAP•	aqua3 OS Explorer 131 Romsey, Andover & Test Valley
•START / FINISH•	Grid reference: SU 308530
•DOG FRIENDLINESS•	Keep dogs under control at all times
•PARKING•	Lower Chute Club
•PUBLIC TOILETS•	None on route

BACKGROUND TO THE WALK

This walk explores the hilly and relatively deserted border country between Wiltshire and Hampshire, in what remains of Chute Forest. In medieval times vast tracts of woodland canopied an area stretching from Savernake Forest, in the north, to Salisbury, in the south, before swelling out again into the New Forest, providing a prime hunting ground for Norman and medieval kings.

The Chutes

The parishes of Chute and Chute Forest can be traced back to Norman times and it is believed that the ancient meaning of Chute is wood or forest. Habitation within the parishes at that time may well have been no more than a few cottages in a large clearing occupied by charcoal burners or peasants. Deforestation began in 1632 during the reign of Charles I (1600–49), who divided the area up among his favoured nobles. The result of this is still evident today, for there is no village in the generally accepted sense of the word, but a collection of five small hamlets – Upper and Lower Chute, Chute Standen, Chute Forest and Chute Cadley – which developed around what were once farms or country houses, such as Standen House and Chute Lodge.

The landscape is still well wooded with a mixture of copse, plantations, windbreaks or 'rows' and roadside plantings of beech linked by a sprinkling of hedgerow trees. The paths and byways you will follow on this walk explore in depth this quite remote area of Wiltshire, which rises to over 800ft (244m), affording splendid views south across Hampshire to the Isle of Wight.

The highest point of the walk is on the impressive Chute Causeway, which was originally part of the Roman highway from Winchester, in Hampshire, to Mildenhall, near Marlborough. It forms a great arc around some of the most attractive scenery in Wiltshire, for just north of the now paved road are deep combes and steep hills (such as Knolls Down). Some of these are so steep that the Roman road, which usually ignores natural obstacles, swerves to avoid the deep combe, known as Hippenscombe Bottom. At the eastern end of the Causeway is Conholt House, a large, early 19th-century building of grey brick. It was here during excavations in 1898, that a small terrace set with 12–16 inches (30–40cm) of flint, covered with layers of soil, clay and compacted chalk, was uncovered. Part of this terrrace appears to have been burned, which offers an explanation as to how the Romans built such straight roads – by lighting fires at both ends of the semi-circular section of the Causeway they could line up the columns of smoke to align their road.

Walk 1 Directions

① Turn left out of the car park and then right at the T-junction. Fork left at the **war memorial**, then turn left again by the 'Chute Cadley' village sign. Keep left and take the bridle path, a track, through the edge of woodland. Continue between hedgerows and descend into **Chute Standen**.

Walk 1

② Turn right at the T-junction then, where the lane swings left to Standen House, keep straight on up a grassy track of **Breach Lane**. At the T-junction, turn right and then left along the edge of woodland. Continue for ½ mile (800m) to **Chute Causeway**.

③ Cross straight over the causeway and steeply descend the track to a metalled lane in **Hippenscombe Bottom**. Turn left, then right through a gate and swing right, then left between farm buildings. Fork right along a grassy track, which soon swings left and steadily ascend to a crossing of ways.

④ Turn sharp right along the gravel track. At **Fosbury Farm**, bear right and walk beside woodland. Follow the track into the woods and soon pass through the ancient earthworks into **Fosbury Ring** on top of Knolls Down.

⑤ Fork left, exit the ring and walk down the left-hand field edge. Go through the gap in the corner and maintain direction around the edge

of a large field. Descend to a cottage in the corner. Turn right along the lane and cross the stile almost immediately on your left. Keep to the right-hand field edge to a stile and lane and turn right into **Vernham Dean**.

⑥ Take the waymarked track beside a house called **Underwood**. Follow the left-hand field edge, then just before a gap in the corner, turn right down a hedged track. Follow the track just within woodland, then follow the waymarker steeply uphill across a field and through a small plantation to a stile. Turn left along the top of the escarpment to a gate in the corner and the road.

⑦ Turn right then, where the road swings sharp left by a junction, keep straight on over another stile. Initially head towards a barn, but then fork left across a depression and continue to another stile. Cross the next field to a stile and walk down a track between fields. Bear slightly left, then walk along the right-hand field edge to cross a stile by a cattle grid.

⑧ Keep to the right-hand edge of a long field and cross the stile on the right just before the corner. Continue beside woodland, eventually joining a drive which becomes a metalled lane. Turn right at the T-junction and soon retrace your steps back to the **car park**.

Great Bedwyn and the Kennet and Avon Canal

Combine a peaceful walk beside the Kennet and Avon Canal with a visit to Wiltshire's only working windmill and the beam engines at Crofton.

•DISTANCE•	5½ miles (8.8km)
•MINIMUM TIME•	2hrs
•ASCENT / GRADIENT•	147ft (45m) ▲ ▲ ▲
•LEVEL OF DIFFICULTY•	👫 👫 👫
•PATHS•	Field paths, woodland tracks, tow path, roads, 1 stile
•LANDSCAPE•	Farmland, woodland, canal and village scenery
•SUGGESTED MAP•	aqua3 OS Explorer 157 Marlborough & Savernake Forest
•START / FINISH•	Grid reference: SU 279645
•DOG FRIENDLINESS•	Dogs can be off lead along tow path
•PARKING•	Great Bedwyn Station
•PUBLIC TOILETS•	Crofton Pumping Station, portaloo at Wilton Windmill

BACKGROUND TO THE WALK

Situated beside a peaceful stretch of the Kennet and Avon Canal, the large village of Great Bedwyn was formerly a market town, with borough status from the 11th century until the Reform Act of 1832, it even returned two Members of Parliament. It still has the appearance of a small town with a wide main street, continuous rows of cottages, a few elegant town houses and the flint Church of St Mary the Virgin, one of the largest and finest churches in the area, set in low lying land close to the canal.

Kennet and Avon Canal

Undeniably, the main reason most visitors come to Great Bedwyn is to enjoy the sights and sounds of the Kennet and Avon Canal and the beautiful scenery it meanders through south west of the village. It was in 1788 that the idea of linking the River Kennet, which flows into the Thames at Reading, with the River Avon at Bath by means of an artificial waterway was first mooted. The navigation between the rivers had to rise to 450ft (137m) and then descend on the other side and needed 104 locks, two aqueducts and, at the summit, a tunnel over 500yds (457m) long. Construction on the ambitious project, designed by John Rennie (1761–1821), started in 1794 and was completed in 1810. The canal was used to carry vast quantities of coal from the Somerset coalfield, iron, stone and slate, local agricultural products and timber, and to bring luxuries like tobacco and spirits from London to Bath, Bristol and the intervening towns.

Decline and Restoration

Transporting goods along the canal proved successful for 40 years then, with the completion of the railways offering faster and more efficient transport, the canal began to fall into decline. Since 1962 the Kennet and Avon Canal Trust and British Waterways have revitalised the navigable waterway by clearing the waters and locks for leisure barges and making the banks and tow paths accessible to anglers, naturalists and walkers.

Also part of the restoration scheme, and the highlight of your walk along the tow path, are the magnificent beam engines at Crofton Pumping Station. The two beam engines, the 1812 Boulton and Watt and the 1845 Harvey of Hale, operate a huge cast-iron beam and were used to raise water from Wilton Water to the summit level of the canal. Beautifully restored and powered by steam from a hand-stoked, coal-fired Lancashire boiler, you may be lucky to see them working if you're visiting on a summer weekend.

Wilton Windmill
The county's only complete surviving working windmill stands proudly on a chalk hilltop overlooking the canal. Built in 1821, after the construction of the canal had diverted the water previously used to power mills, it is a five-storey brick tower mill and was fully operational until the 1890s. It closed and became derelict in the 1920s. Restored in the 1970s and floodlit at night, you can once again see local corn being ground into flour.

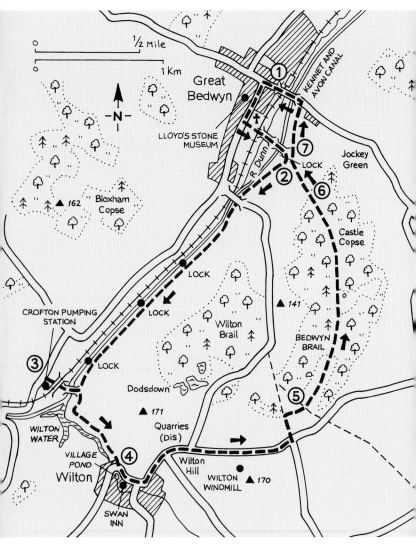

Walk 2

Walk 2 Directions

① Walk back to the main road in Great Bedwyn and turn right, then left down **Church Street**. Pass **Lloyd's Stone Museum** and the church, then take the footpath left between the two graveyards. Climb a stile, cross a field to a kissing gate, then carefully cross the railway line to a further kissing gate. Cross the footbridge, then the bridge over the **Kennet and Avon Canal** and descend to the tow path.

> **WHAT TO LOOK FOR** ⓘ
> In **St Mary's Church**, Great Bedwyn, look for the tomb of Sir John Seymour in the chancel. His daughter Jane was Henry VIII's third and best loved wife.

② Turn right, pass beneath the bridge and continue along the tow path for 1½ miles (2.4km), passing three locks, to reach **Lock 60**. Cross the canal here, turn left, then follow a wooded path right and pass through the tunnel beneath the railway. Ascend steps to the **Crofton Pumping Station**.

③ Retrace your steps back to the tow path and Lock 60. Take the footpath right, waymarked to Wilton Windmill, and walk beside **Wilton Water** along the edge of fields. Eventually, turn right down a short track to a lane by the village pond in **Wilton**.

> **WHERE TO EAT AND DRINK** ⓘ
> Great Bedwyn has two pubs, the **Cross Keys** and the **Three Tuns**, and a bakery. Light refreshments are available if visiting the **Crofton Beam Engines**, while at Wilton, the homely **Swan Inn** offers decent doorstop sandwiches, home-cooked pub dishes, good Sunday lunches and a selection of real ales.

④ Turn left, then just past the **Swan Inn**, follow the lane left, signed 'Great Bedwyn'. Climb out of the village and fork right to pass **Wilton Windmill**. Continue along the lane and turn left on to a track, opposite the lane to Marten. Just before the wooded track snakes downhill, turn right along a bridle path (unsigned) beside woodland.

⑤ At a staggered crossing of paths, turn right, then in 50yds (46m), turn left, signed 'Great Bedwyn'. Proceed down a well-surfaced track and go through a gate into **Bedwyn Brail**. Continue though the woods, following signs to Great Bedwyn. Go straight across a clearing before forking left to re-enter the woods in the left-hand corner of the clearing.

⑥ On emerging in a field corner, keep left along the field boundary, go through a gap in the hedge and descend along the left-hand side of the next field, with **Great Bedwyn** visible ahead. Near the bottom of the field, bear half-right, downhill to the canal.

⑦ Pass through a gate by a bridge and **Lock 64** and turn right along the tow path. Go through the car park to the road, then turn left over the canal and rail bridges before turning right back to **Great Bedwyn Station**.

> **WHILE YOU'RE THERE** ⓘ
> Visit **Lloyd's Stone Museum** in Great Bedwyn, a fascinating little open-air museum that demonstrates the art of stonemasonry. Here you can see monuments, gravestones and sculpture dating back to the 18th century. Just north of Great Bedwyn is **Chisbury Camp**, an ancient hill fort with the ruins of a 13th-century chapel standing within its 50ft (15m) high earth ramparts.

Savernake's Royal Forest

A walk through an ancient forest landscape and beside a tranquil canal.

•DISTANCE•	5½ miles (8.8km)
•MINIMUM TIME•	2hrs 30min
•ASCENT / GRADIENT•	213ft (65m) ▲▲▲
•LEVEL OF DIFFICULTY•	🚶 🚶 🚶
•PATHS•	Woodland tracks, tow path, bridle paths, country lanes
•LANDSCAPE•	Forest, farmland, canal
•SUGGESTED MAP•	aqua3 OS Explorer 157 Marlborough & Savernake Forest
•START / FINISH•	Grid reference: SU 215646
•DOG FRIENDLINESS•	Dogs can be off lead through Savernake Forest and along tow path
•PARKING•	Hat Gate 8 picnic area off A346 south of Marlborough
•PUBLIC TOILETS•	None on route

BACKGROUND TO THE WALK

Situated on an undulating chalk plateau high above Marlborough on the extreme north east edge of Salisbury Plain, Savernake consists of 2,300 acres (931.5ha) of mixed woodland managed by the Forestry Commission. In the Middle Ages, Savernake was a wilderness of bracken and heathland stretching for miles across the Wiltshire countryside and had been a royal hunting ground from long before the Norman Conquest. It was William the Conqueror (1027–87) who appointed the first hereditary warden, Richard Esturmy, and subsequent kings of England rode through the forest glades in pursuit of deer, which were in plentiful supply for the royal sport.

The Seymours

In the 15th century a daughter of the Esturmy family married into the Seymour family who then became wardens of Savernake. It was in 1535 that Jane Seymour, daughter of Sir John Seymour, was first introduced to King Henry VIII while he was hunting with Sir John in the forest. Local tradition has it that Henry VIII married Jane at Savernake, where a great barn was hung with tapestries and transformed into a banqueting hall for the wedding feast. Jane's brother, Edward Seymour, became warden in 1536 and was later created Protector of the Realm, the Duke of Somerset, on Henry VIII's death in 1547. He managed to persuade King Edward to transfer the ownership of Savernake from the Crown to the Seymour family. In 1676 it passed by marriage to the Bruce family and so to the present owner, the Marquis of Ailesbury, whose mansion, the present Tottenham House, was begun in 1781 by the first Earl of Ailesbury.

18th-century Landscaping

Although a large part of the forest was enclosed during the early 17th century, much of Savernake decayed due to the lack of systematic replanting following increased timber demands for shipbuilding. Few trees were declared fit for building use by a naval surveyor in 1675. Today's forest of grand oaks, chestnuts and stately beeches was the inspiration of landscape gardener 'Capability' Brown (1715–83). He planned the 4 mile (6.4km) long

Grand Avenue that cuts north to south through the forest, and the eight lesser beech avenues which lead to its centre. Originally intended to be very formal, it now has an air of informality, with young broad-leaved trees and glorious tall pines intermingling with the surviving great beeches and ancient pollarded oaks.

Column Ride

You will experience the grandeur of this beautiful forest as you journey down one of the deliciously cool and shady rides to the Ailesbury Monument, an elegant classical column standing at the end of Column Ride, a straight 2 mile (3.2km) ride that extends to Tottenham House. The column was built by Thomas Bruce in memory of his uncle, Charles Bruce, a former Earl of Ailesbury, who 'left to him these estates and procured for him the barony of Tottenham'. The inscription also refers to George III who conferred upon Thomas Bruce the honour of an earldom.

Walk 3

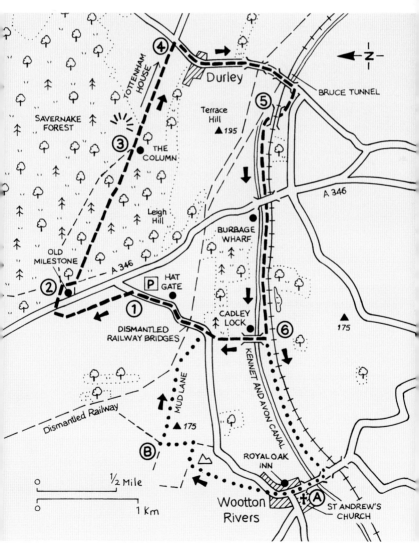

Walk 3

Walk 3 Directions

① From the car park, turn right, then almost immediately left past a wooden barrier. Follow the wooded path for 500yds (457m), then bear right to reach the **A346**. Cross over near an old milestone and take the track beyond a wooden barrier, signed to **Tottenham House**.

② In 150yds (137m), at a major crossing of routes, turn right and after a similar distance at a more minor crossing of paths, turn left. Follow this straight track (which can be very muddy in places) for ¾ mile (1.2km) to **The Column**.

WHERE TO EAT AND DRINK ⓘ

The 16th-century, thatched and timber-framed **Royal Oak Inn** at Wootton Rivers on Walk 4 offers a good range of interesting pub food, real ales and a sun-trap courtyard. If hungry and thirsty, it is well worth undertaking the extra few miles as Walk 3 is devoid of a refreshment stop.

---

③ Maintain direction towards Tottenham House, which is visible in the distance. On leaving the woodland, continue along a wide fenced track, eventually reaching a gate and road opposite the drive to **Tottenham House**.

④ Turn right, walk through the hamlet of **Durley** and keep to the lane across the old railway bridge, then the main railway bridge, and shortly take the footpath on the right, waymarked '**Wootton Rivers**'. You are now walking above the Kennet and Avon Canal as it passes through the **Bruce Tunnel**.

WHILE YOU'RE THERE

Drive east towards Great Bedwyn to see the magnificent steam-powered beam engines at **Crofton Pumping Station** or visit Wiltshire's only operating windmill at Wilton (► Walk 2). If heading north towards Marlborough, lookout for the **Big Belly Oak**, one of Savernake's oldest trees, set right beside the A346.

---

⑤ Walk down some steps, pass through a narrow and low tunnel under the railway line and join the canal tow path just below the entrance to the **Bruce Tunnel**. Turn left along the tow path for about 1½ miles (2.4km), passing beneath the **A346** at **Burbage Wharf** to reach **Cadley Lock**.

⑥ Turn right over **bridge No 105** and follow the metalled track to a T-junction. Turn right and keep to the road, passing two dismantled railway bridges, back to the car park at **Hat Gate**.

WHAT TO LOOK FOR ⓘ

You may catch a glimpse of **fallow deer**, with fan-shaped antlers and spotted summer coats, slipping silently into a thicket as you walk through Savernake Forest. Well-lit clearings may be carpeted with primroses and the woods with bluebells, while wood anemones, wood sorrel and rosebay willowherb thrive in spring and early summer. As you cross the A346, note the old **milestone** in the hedge, 'To Tottenham House 2 miles, 3 furlongs and 143 yards. To Marlborough Town Hall, 2 miles, 7 furlongs and 70 yards'.

Wootton Rivers

Continue along the tow path to Wootton Rivers and a charming pub.
See map and information panel for Walk 3

•DISTANCE•	7¼ miles (11.7km)
•MINIMUM TIME•	4hrs
•ASCENT / GRADIENT•	279ft (85m) ▲▲ ▲
•LEVEL OF DIFFICULTY•	🚶 🚶 🚶

Walk 4 Directions (Walk 3 option)

At Point ⑥, don't cross the bridge, instead keep to the canal tow path and pass three further locks to reach **bridge No 108** at **Wootton Rivers**. Leave the tow path and turn right across the bridge into the village.

The section of the Kennet and Avon Canal from Wootton Rivers to the western portal of the Bruce Tunnel includes the Wootton Rivers flight of four locks, which raise the canal 35ft (11m) to its summit level of 450ft (137m) compared to 65ft (20m) in Bath. Beyond the 502ft (153m) long Bruce Tunnel and Crofton Pumping Station, the canal descends gradually all the way to the Thames at Reading.

Wootton Rivers is a classic Wiltshire village. Essentially a linear settlement, it is particularly pretty with its mile long (1.6km) main street composed almost entirely of timber-framed, thatched cottages and brick houses. As you stroll gently uphill away from the canal and its restored lock and keeper's cottage, take the long enclosed pathway on your left to visit

St Andrew's Church, which stands close to the impressive manor house. Of particular interest is the clock in the wooden belfry. Built in 1911 to commemorate the Coronation of George V, it is unique in having three faces, two are conventional, the third displays the words 'Glory be to God' around the edge of the dial instead of numerals. It was designed by the amusingly named Jack Spratt, an eccentric countryman and amateur clockmaker, out of donations of mechanical junk, old prams, bicycles and bedsteads as the people of the village could not afford to buy one. It is said to have a repertoire of 24 chimes.

Pass **St Andrew's Church**, Point Ⓐ, on your left and the **Royal Oak Inn** on your right then, as the road swings right, take the waymarked bridle path left by the house called **Martinsell**. Follow this tree-lined track, which gently climbs to a T-junction of routes at the top of the hill. Turn right then, in the field corner, turn left and in 50yds (46m) join the track on your right. Turn left and ascend to a further T-junction, Point Ⓑ. Turn right down **Mud Lane**, a wooded track, eventually reaching a metalled lane in ½ mile (800m). Turn left along the lane back to **Hat Gate** car park.

Ramsbury and a Murder

A gentle walk through the tranquil Kennet Valley to Littlecote House.

•DISTANCE•	5 miles (8km)
•MINIMUM TIME•	2hrs
•ASCENT / GRADIENT•	229ft (70m) ▲▲▲
•LEVEL OF DIFFICULTY•	👫 👫 👫
•PATHS•	Field paths and established tracks
•LANDSCAPE•	Farmland, woodland, parkland, village streets
•SUGGESTED MAP•	aqua3 OS Explorers 157 Marlborough & Savernake; 158 Newbury & Hungerford
•START / FINISH•	Grid reference: SU 274715 (on Explorer 157)
•DOG FRIENDLINESS•	Keep dogs under control at all times
•PARKING•	Ample roadside parking in Ramsbury
•PUBLIC TOILETS•	None on route

Walk 5 Directions

The large old village of Ramsbury nestles on a wide stretch of the River Kennet close to the Berkshire border. Between AD 908 and 1058 Ramsbury was the centre of a flourishing diocese, complete with cathedral and bishop, before it was transferred to preferred Sherborne and later to Old Sarum. Although a mere parish for over nine centuries, the village has an impressive church built on Anglo-Saxon foundations and many fine Jacobean and Georgian buildings, notably Ramsbury Manor, a handsome brick building of nine bays, built in 1680 by John Webb, son-in-law of Inigo Jones, that takes advantage of its fine riverside setting. It was in this house that Oliver Cromwell (1599–1658) laid his plans for the subjugation of Ireland

From the **Square** and the **Bell Inn**, take **Scholards Lane** signed to Hungerford. At **The Knap** turn right, signed 'Froxfield', cross the

River Kennet and, just before a cottage, take the metalled track left, waymarked to **Littlecote House**. As the drive bears right, continue straight on along a track through the valley. In ½ mile (800m), pass a cottage called **West Lodge**, and enter a field. Keep left along the field edge, eventually passing the remains of a Roman villa.

William George, the steward of Littlecote Park, unearthed the remains of the villa, including a large mosaic floor, in the early 18th century. Edward Popham, the owner of Littlecote, allowed George to make detailed drawings of the mosaic before ordering it to be buried again to avoid publicity.

> **WHILE YOU'RE THERE** ⓘ
> Follow the walk with a leisurely drive to the attractive market town of **Marlborough**. A borough since 1204, it has a very wide main street lined with some fine 18th-century houses. The famous Polly Tea Rooms is the perfect post-walk refreshment destination as it offers irresistible set afternoon teas.

George died shortly afterwards and it was thought that the mosaic had subsequently been destroyed until it was rediscovered by archaeologists in 1978.

Excavations have continued over the 3 acre (1.2ha) site but you will find the showpiece of the villa, the superb Orpheus mosaic, beautifully restored and relaid in its original position. Constructed in around AD 360, it plays an important role in our understanding of early Christian architecture.

Continue through the grounds of **Littlecote House**. The right of way soon passes in front of the house and down the avenue of trees to the gatehouse and road.

Built between 1490 and 1520, Littlecote is an exquisite manor house standing amidst spacious lawns and gardens, with the River Kennet running through the surrounding parkland. Behind the building's long, gabled façade are some fine architectural treasures, notably the 110ft (33.5m) Long Gallery, the oak-panelled Great Hall, and the magnificent Cromwellian chapel, probably the only complete example of its kind in England.

Tales of mystery, intrigue and royal visits abound at Littlecote, now an adults-only hotel. Jane Seymour is said to have entertained Henry VIII here before their marriage. Later, Charles II dined here with Colonel Alexander Popham. In 1688 William of Orange met with the commissioners of King James II at the house. Among the regular sightings of ghosts have been that of a mother and her baby, a midwife and that of Will Darrell who owned

the estate in the mid-16th century. Known as 'Wild' Darrell for his unruly lifestyle, it is said that he had many mistresses, including his own sister whom he made pregnant. One night he called for Mother Barnes, a midwife, to deliver the child. She was brought blindfolded into a secret chamber off the Long Gallery, delivered the child and gave it to Darrell who immediately threw it on the fire. Although rewarded with gold, the midwife's conscience troubled her and she finally told the local magistrate. Darrell was brought to trial, accused of murder, before Judge Popham but was aquitted after bribing Popham with the offer of Littlecote House. A year later Darrell was killed falling from his horse.

Turn right, ascend the narrow lane then, where it turns sharp left, keep straight on through gates, signed '**Ramsbury**'. As the metalled track swings right, proceed straight ahead along the gravelled track. At a junction of tracks, fork right along a concrete track, following the bridle path uphill. Where the concrete track swings right into woodland near the top of the hill, take the path ahead just within the woodland fringe. The path soon veers right and descends into the valley, soon to follow the left-hand edge of a field to reach the track and cottage encountered on the outward route. Retrace your steps back into **Ramsbury**.

WHERE TO EAT AND DRINK ⓘ

The best of the three pubs in Ramsbury is the **Bell,** which overlooks the Square. Well refurbished, it provides a stylish and innovative menu and simpler, yet equally appetising lunchtime bar meals. Good changing ales, decent wines and a sheltered rear garden.

Walk 6

Clarendon's Lost Palace

Explore ancient woodland for the remains of Clarendon Palace.

•**DISTANCE**•	7½ miles (12.1km)
•**MINIMUM TIME**•	3hrs
•**ASCENT / GRADIENT**•	410ft (125m) ▲▲▲
•**LEVEL OF DIFFICULTY**•	👫 👫 👫
•**PATHS**•	Field paths, woodland tracks, country lanes, 9 stiles
•**LANDSCAPE**•	Gently undulating farmland and woodland
•**SUGGESTED MAP**•	aqua3 OS Explorer 130 Salisbury & Stonehenge
•**START / FINISH**•	Grid reference: SU 212312
•**DOG FRIENDLINESS**•	Keep dogs under control across farmland
•**PARKING**•	Pitton village hall
•**PUBLIC TOILETS**•	None on route

BACKGROUND TO THE WALK

The parish of Pitton and Farley lies on the boundary of a vast estate, Clarendon Park, which occupies a wide arc of country due east of Salisbury. In Saxon times the area was covered with an ancient forest and within its bounds are the remains of the once magnificent Clarendon Palace, which began its life as a Saxon hunting lodge. It was expanded by the Plantagenets into a great country house becoming, in the 14th century, second only to the Palace of Westminster in size and importance.

Royal Residence

Henry II and Henry III were both responsible for creating this grand building with its great hall, lavish apartments, council chambers and chapels, all beautifully adorned with wall-paintings and floor tiles. Many great names in history visited the palace as a place of retreat and pleasure, notably Thomas Beckett and the captive kings, John of France and David of Scotland, who hunted with their captor, King Edward III, in the surrounding forests.

The palace continued to be an occasional residence of the royal family until the outbreak of the War of the Roses in 1455. At the end of the conflict in 1485, although in decline, the palace was sustained and occasionally visited by Yorkist, Tudor and Stuart monarchs until the land and the now almost ruined building was confiscated by Parliament in the wake of the execution of Charles I in 1649.

The archaeologist Dr Tancred Borenius excavated the site during the 1930s revealing evidence of a Saxon building below Norman foundations. He also identified the great hall, the kitchens, the royal quarters and several council chambers. Until recently, very little could be seen, except for a few ruined walls and broken floors lying only a few paces from the Clarendon Way. You can now view the results of the on-going excavations that are once again beginning to reveal the hidden history and glory of this once magnificent palace.

Just south of Pitton is the village of Farley, a fragmented settlement built around a triangle of lanes with a pleasant assortment of buildings. It is known for its classical church, built of country brick in a style influenced by Sir Christopher Wren. It was built for Sir Stephen Fox who was born in the village of poor parentage, but being an able and intelligent man he served Charles II, eventually rising to the post of Paymaster General.

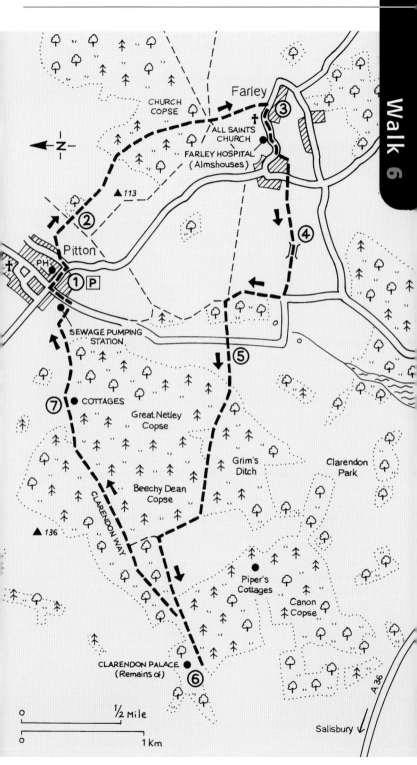

Farley

CHURCH
COPSE

ALL SAINTS
CHURCH

FARLEY HOSPITAL
(Almshouses)

③

Pitton

④

PH

② ▲ 113

① P

SEWAGE PUMPING
STATION

⑤

⑦ ● COTTAGES

Great Netley
Copse

Grim's
Ditch

Clarendon
Park

Beechy Dean
Copse

CLARENDON WAY

▲ 136

Piper's
Cottages

Canon
Copse

CLARENDON PALACE
(Remains of)

⑥

½ Mile

1 Km

Salisbury ↓

A36

He later contributed £13,000 (then a huge sum of money) to the building of Chelsea Hospital and in doing so became a friend of Wren. Fox later bought Farley Manor and employed Alexander Fort, an architect who had worked with Wren, to build the handsome village church between 1689 and 1690. The interior has simple panelling and pews, a broad central aisle, some fine monuments and classical-style window glass, giving it an atmosphere and appearance more often found in some London churches.

Walk 6 **Directions**

① From the car park, cross the lane and walk up a cul-de sac to the right of the pub. In 100yds (91m), take the footpath right, heading uphill between houses to a stile. Proceed across a narrow field to a stile, then go ahead along the right-hand field edge to a stile and gate.

② Cross the track and continue along another track to the right of woodland. It narrows to a path and soon reaches a stile and enters **Church Copse**. Where the fenced path joins a track bear right then, at a junction on the woodland fringe, keep straight on downhill into **Farley** village.

> **WHERE TO EAT AND DRINK** ⓘ
> Refresh yourself before or after the walk at the **Silver Plough** in Pitton. It offers an extensive range of home-made food prepared from local produce.

③ At the road, turn right and pass **All Saints Church** and the almshouses. Leave the village and, just before the 30mph sign, cross the stile on the left and follow the hedge right to a stile to the rear of a bungalow. Walk down the drive, cross the lane to a gate and follow the path through a narrow field to a stile and gate.

④ Cross the footbridge and stile ahead, then proceed across the next field, (on the left of power cables),

to a stile and gate. Take the track immediately right and follow this byway to a crossing of tracks. Turn left alongside a fenced enclosure and, on emerging from the wood, head straight across two fields and enter further woodland.

⑤ Walk through the woodland alongside a clearing to your right, and cross a lane back into woodland. Leave the wood and follow the track right, then left around the field edge and soon re-enter the wood. Keep ahead where the **Clarendon Way** merges from the right and continue to the ruins of **Clarendon Palace**.

⑥ From the palace remains, retrace your steps through the wood, this time keeping left along the **Clarendon Way**. Follow the path for nearly a mile (1.6km) through the wood. On emerging, keep straight on down the track and cross the lane by a barn.

⑦ Pass beside cottages and woodland to your right, then walk down a fenced path, soon to follow the diverted footpath signs to the sewage pumping station. At the lane turn left, then right, back to the village hall.

> **WHAT TO LOOK FOR**
> Having visited Farley's fine classical church, note the brick-built, long and low **Farley Hospital Almshouses**, built by Alexander Fort in 1681, for Sir Stephen Fox, ten years before he built the church.

Amesbury and the Woodford Valley

Catch a glimpse of Stonehenge on this downland and riverside ramble.

•DISTANCE•	6½ miles (10.4km)
•MINIMUM TIME•	3hrs
•ASCENT / GRADIENT•	518ft (158m) ▲▲▲
•LEVEL OF DIFFICULTY•	🚶🚶 🚶🚶 🚶🚶
•PATHS•	Tracks, field and bridle paths, roads, 3 stiles
•LANDSCAPE•	River valley and chalk downland
•SUGGESTED MAP•	aqua3 OS Explorer 130 Salisbury & Stonehenge
•START / FINISH•	Grid reference: SU 149411
•DOG FRIENDLINESS•	Keep dogs on lead through villages and water-meadows
•PARKING•	Free parking at Amesbury Recreation Ground car park
•PUBLIC TOILETS•	Amesbury

BACKGROUND TO THE WALK

Amesbury is a pleasant market town set in a bend of the River Avon, which is crossed by a five-arched bridge built in Palladian style. Its proximity to the eastern edge of Salisbury Plain means that the neighbourhood is dominated by large military camps and their personnel, including the experimental flying base of Boscombe Down. Despite this intrusion, the lesser-known chalk downland and the beautiful Woodford Valley to the south of the town remain delightfully unspoilt. Criss-crossed by breezy byways and tranquil riverside paths, this is perfect walking country, rich in archaeological treasures, such as Bronze Age barrows and Stonehenge, Wiltshire's most famous prehistoric monument, with the valleys dotted with chocolate-box villages filled with idyllic thatched cottages.

Amesbury Abbey

According to legend, Amesbury was founded by an uncle of King Arthur, a Roman Briton named Ambrosius Aurelianus, hence the name Amesbury. After Arthur's death in the 6th century, it is said that Queen Guinevere sought refuge in the Wessex region, probably retreating to Amesbury Abbey. The abbey was succeeded in AD 979 by a nunnery which eventually became the richest in England. It achieved fame as the refuge of Mary, daughter of Edward I, and her grandmother Queen Eleanor, Henry III's widow. After the Dissolution of the Monasteries in 1540, the convent was demolished and a house was built on the site. This was replaced in 1661 by a new mansion, designed by John Webb in the style of Inigo Jones, his father-in-law. Here, the handsome and hospitable Duchess of Queensberry inspired John Gay to write *The Beggar's Opera* (1728).

The present Amesbury Abbey was rebuilt in 1840 by Thomas Hopper for Sir Edward Antrobus, owner of the Stonehenge Estate. Although now a nursing home, you can see the colonnaded front from the impressive neoclassical entrance in Church Street. Amesbury's ancient and atmospheric church is all that remains of the original abbey. Built by the Saxons and remodelled by the Normans, it has a fine example of an early 14th-century window in the chancel, striking tracery and carved bosses.

The meandering River Avon threads its way south from Amesbury for 7 miles (11.3km), flowing through the Woodford Valley to Salisbury in the Avon Valley. Peaceful and protected, it is the unspoilt setting for some of Wiltshire's finest villages, notably the three Woodfords and Great Durnford, the quintessential English village. With its converted mill, where weeping willows dip into the crystal clear waters of the Avon, picture-postcard thatched cottages with flower-filled gardens, an impressive Norman church and its handsome manor house, you will find Great Durnford a delight to stroll through. Take time to visit the church and, if the pub is open, relax with a pint in the garden which overlooks the lush water-meadows.

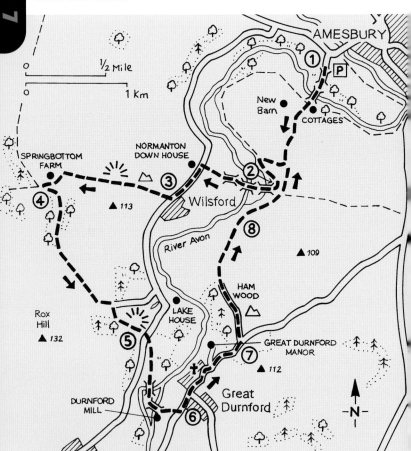

Walk 7 Directions

① Take the footpath to the right of the play area, cross a footbridge and bear right to cross the main footbridge over the **River Avon**. At a crossing of tracks, take the track signed 'Durnford' and pass to the right of cottages. Head uphill to a junction and proceed straight on, downhill to a gate. Turn right along the field edge and bear left in the corner to join a path through the valley bottom beside a stream.

② Shortly, cross a footbridge on your right and follow the path

Walk 7

WHAT TO LOOK FOR

As you climb up the downs away from Wilsford you will be rewarded with a distant view of **Stonehenge** and the extensive prehistoric landscape of Normanton Down, littered with earthworks and burial mounds. **Lake House**, a 16th-century mansion built by a wealthy clothier, and now home to Sting, the rock musician.

through marshy ground to cross a bridge over the Avon. Bear right over a small bridge and keep left through a paddock beside the thatched cob wall of **Normanton Down House** to a stile. Bear right along the drive to the road. Turn left then, in ¼ mile (400m), turn right up the farm road towards **Springbottom Farm**.

③ Either walk up the tarmac road or join the path through the spinney on your right, the latter affording cameo views across **Normanton Down** to **Stonehenge**. Pass barns and descend to the farm complex. Just beyond the barns, bear left with a red byway arrow on to a track beside paddocks.

④ Keep to this track through the downland valley (**Lake Bottom**) for ¾ mile (1.2km). Where it becomes metalled at Lake, take the arrowed path right, up the left-hand edge of a field into woodland and bear left uphill to a stile. Keep right along the field edge, with views left to **Lake House**, to a further stile.

⑤ Cross the lane and take the bridle path right in front of a thatched house. Head downhill, cross a drive and bear left to cross two footbridges over the Avon. Pass beside **Durnford Mill** and follow the drive out to the lane.

⑥ Turn left and walk through **Great Durnford**, passing the church and drive to **Great Durnford Manor**, following the lane right, uphill through woodland. Descend and take the waymarked bridle path left beside a house.

WHERE TO EAT AND DRINK

The **Black Horse** in Great Durnford is a traditional free house offering a range of ales and a varied bar menu. Amesbury has several cafés and pubs, including the **Friar Tuck** café, the **Kings Arms**, the **New Inn** and the **Antrobus Arms**.

⑦ Steeply ascend through the edge of **Ham Wood**. On leaving the wood, bear off right along a narrow path through scrub to a gate. Keep right along the edge of two large fields to a gate.

⑧ Maintain your direction through the pastureland, soon to bear off right across the field towards a waymarker post at the field boundary. Ignore the public footpath to the right, signed to Stockport, and walk down the field edge to a gate to rejoin your outward route. Retrace your steps back into **Amesbury**.

WHILE YOU'RE THERE

Two miles (3.2km) west of Amesbury (off the A303) stands **Stonehenge**, the most famous prehistoric monument in Europe, a World Heritage Site of major importance surrounded by remains of ceremonial and domestic structures. Enjoy an audio tour and discover the history and legends which surround this unique stone circle. Sadly, in the interests of conservation, you'll have to view it from a distance, which will really disappoint enthusiasts. Less busy and pre-dating Stonehenge is **Woodhenge** (off the A345 north of Amesbury), once a ritual temple aligned with sunrise on Midsummer Day.

Avon Valley from Downton

Discover Downton's architectural heritage and an 18th-century estate associated with Lord Nelson.

•DISTANCE•	5 miles (8km)
•MINIMUM TIME•	3hrs
•ASCENT / GRADIENT•	229ft (70m) ▲ ▲ ▲
•LEVEL OF DIFFICULTY•	🚶 🚶 🚶
•PATHS•	Riverside paths, downland tracks, metalled lanes, 6 stiles
•LANDSCAPE•	River valley, woodland, downland pasture, village streets
•SUGGESTED MAP•	aqua3 OS Explorers 130 Salisbury & Stonehenge; 131 Romsey, Andover & Test Valley
•START / FINISH•	Grid reference: SU 180214 (on Explorer 130)
•DOG FRIENDLINESS•	Keep dogs under control across pasture
•PARKING•	Plenty of roadside parking in High Street
•PUBLIC TOILETS•	None on route

BACKGROUND TO THE WALK

Close to the Hampshire border and straddling the channels of the River Avon south of Salisbury, Downton has the air of a small town about it. Despite this, the central area, known as The Borough, with its wide and pretty green and thatched timber-framed cottages, has not lost its village feel. This is the medieval Downton built as a 'new town' by the Bishop of Winchester around 1205, close to The Moot an earthwork that was once the site of a palace built in 1138 by Henry de Blois for the Bishops of Winchester. Gracing this historic plot is Moot House, an 18th-century mansion set in landscaped grounds that include an amphitheatre, lily pond and viewpoint. Near by stands the Manor House, formerly the parsonage, an Elizabethan house once owned by the Raleigh family.

Downton was made a borough in the 13th century, entitling the town to hold markets and fairs, it supported a mayor and sent two MPs to Parliament between 1395 and 1832. It was a profitable borough as burgesses paid their rents in cash rather than holding land against feudal labour and produce. Downton continued to prosper as industry and commerce flourished. Lace was produced as a cottage industry here, and the village has long been associated with flour- and paper-milling. From 1885 Wiggins, Teape, Carter and Barlow produced handmade paper until the end of the First World War. For centuries the village has supported thriving trout fisheries and today Downton is renowned as an angling centre for the Wiltshire Avon.

Admiral Nelson's House

Having crossed the River Avon east of Charlton All Saints, note the large mansion set in parkland as you traverse a field between woodlands. Dating back to the 18th century, and once known as Standlynch House, it was acquired by the Treasury in 1814 and renamed Trafalgar House after being given to the heirs of Admiral Viscount Nelson, in recognition of the services of Britain's greatest seafaring hero. The Nelson family continued to live here until 1948. Make sure you take the short detour to visit the redundant chapel, once the Nelson family's private chapel, and look for the Nelson name on some of the gravestones.

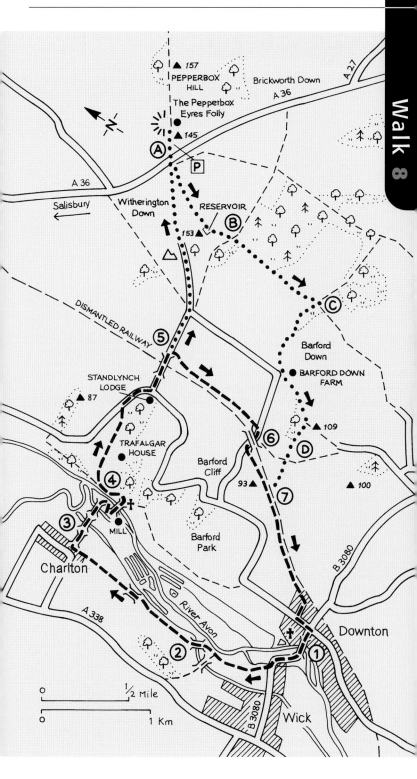

Walk 8 Directions

① Head west along the **High Street**, cross the river bridge and take the gravel footpath right, signed 'Charlton All Saints'. Walk alongside the river, go through a kissing gate and keep to the footpath as it swings away from the river along a causeway through water-meadows. The path widens to a track and as this bears left towards a bridge, fork right along a path to a stile and footbridge.

② Turn right along a concrete track then, as this bears to the left towards farm buildings, fork right across a stile and keep to the right-hand field edge to a small brick bridge and stile. Head straight across the field to a stile and cross the next field to a stile by a house. Cross the gravel drive and stile opposite. Walk beside the hedge on your right, following it left, then continue straight ahead to a public footbridge.

WHAT TO LOOK FOR

Note the intricate form of irrigation, a floating **water-meadow** system, that controlled river flooding by turning it to its advantage, as you head north beside the River Avon from Downton.

---

③ Cross a stile and a further footbridge to join a footpath through reedy marshland. Pass through a gate and then cross a series of footbridges across weirs and streams to reach a mill. Turn left in front of the mill and follow the concrete driveway. In 100yds (91m), take the waymarked footpath sharp left (bear right to the chapel), uphill through woodland, eventually reaching a fork of paths.

④ Take the main path right to a stile on the woodland edge. Bear half-right across a field to a gate, **Trafalgar House** is on your right, and follow the woodland path for ¼ mile (400m) to a metalled lane. Turn right uphill and shortly turn left at the junction opposite a lodge.

⑤ Cross the bridge over the disused railway line and take the arrowed bridle path right (on the longer loop, Walk 9, keep to the lane here). Do not follow the course of the old railway at this point, instead keep to the right-hand edge of two fields to reach a road.

WHERE TO EAT AND DRINK

Retire to the **Bull Hotel** at the western end of the village for traditional pub food and locally-brewed Hopback ales. Alternatively, try the 15th-century **White Horse** along The Borough.

---

⑥ Turn right under the bridge and then left to follow the old embankment. When this peters out, maintain direction over the hill and descend to cross the path where Walk 9 rejoins the main route.

⑦ Descend into the valley and as you start to ascend, take the path to the left of the embankment. Eventually, go through a gap in the hedge at the rear of houses and bear right along a fenced path. Cross a road and continue down the path to a gate. Walk down the drive and turn left back to the **High Street**.

WHILE YOU'RE THERE

Venture 2 miles (3.2km) south across the border into Hampshire to visit **Breamore House**, a handsome Elizabethan manor house containing a fine collection of paintings, china and tapestries, acquired by ten generations of the Hulse family.

Pepperbox Hill

A more strenuous loop takes you high above the Avon Valley.
See map and information panel for Walk 8

•DISTANCE•	7¼ miles (11.7km)
•MINIMUM TIME•	4hrs
•ASCENT / GRADIENT•	410ft (125m) ▲▲▲
•LEVEL OF DIFFICULTY•	🚶🚶 🚶🚶 🚶

Walk 9 Directions (Walk 8 option)

Cross the bridge over the old railway, Point ⑤, and keep to the lane. At the sharp right bend take the middle of three tracks ahead of you. Fork right in 50yds (46m) and begin a long, steady climb up the track. Eventually, follow the wooded track downhill to the **A36**, Point Ⓐ. Cross the road with extreme care and follow the byway ahead, signed '**Pepperbox Hill**'. Access to the folly is via the car park on your right.

Built by Giles Eyre in 1606, the Pepperbox, or Eyre's Folly, is generally regarded as one of the earliest follies in the country. It is hexagonal and brick built, with a pyramidal roof and all the windows have been bricked in on all three levels. It is believed that Eyre was envious of the towers of nearby Longford Castle and built his tower on high ground so he could overlook the castle. Some say it is not a folly at all and that Eyre built it as a hunting viewing stand.

The 24 acre (9.7ha) site on which the Pepperbox stands is one of the finest examples of chalk grassland and scrub mosaic in the county, supporting yew woodland, hawthorn and privet thickets, and juniper. The open areas and glades attract the orange clearwing moth, brimstone and grizzled skipper butterfly, while the colourful grassland in summer supports horseshoe vetch, birdsfoot trefoil, bee orchids and wild thyme.

Retrace your steps across the main road then, at the end of the wooded track, fork left and follow the line of an overhead electricity cable. Walk past an aerial and covered reservoir and head downhill on a gravel track beside woodland. At a T-junction, Point Ⓑ, turn left then almost immediately right, down another track. At a fork, bear right and continue within the edge of the woodland. This soon becomes a track between fields. At the crossing of tracks, Point Ⓒ, turn right and just before reaching a metalled lane, take the track left waymarked 'Road used as Public Path'. Walk past **Barford Down Farm** and ascend the grassy track which soon passes through woodland into a field. Keep left, pass a gate and in 50yds (46m) bear right across the brow of **Barford Down**, Point Ⓓ, on an indistinct path. Descend though a gap in the hedge and in 400yds (366m), turn left at the crossing of paths and join Walk 8 at Point ⑦ to return back to **Downton**.

Vale of Pewsey and Oare Hill

Combine a gentle canalside stroll with a stiff downland climb to the summit of Oare Hill for magnificent views across the Vale of Pewsey.

•**DISTANCE**•	5 miles (8km)
•**MINIMUM TIME**•	2hrs 15min
•**ASCENT / GRADIENT**•	393ft (120m) ▲▲▲
•**LEVEL OF DIFFICULTY**•	🚶🚶 🚶
•**PATHS**•	Tow path, tracks, field paths, lanes, 4 stiles
•**LANDSCAPE**•	Vale of Pewsey and chalk downland
•**SUGGESTED MAP**•	aqua3 OS Explorer 157 Marlborough & Savernake Forest
•**START / FINISH**•	Grid reference: SU 157610
•**DOG FRIENDLINESS**•	Let off lead along tow path
•**PARKING**•	Free car park at Pewsey Wharf
•**PUBLIC TOILETS**•	None on route

Walk 10 Directions

The Vale of Pewsey separates Wiltshire's two principle areas of chalk downland, Salisbury Plain to the south and the Marlborough Downs to the north. Through its heart meanders the Kennet and Avon Canal, the longest and most important of the canals within Wiltshire, built between 1794 and 1810 to link the River Kennet, which flows into the Thames at Reading, with the River Avon at Bath. It was used to carry iron, coal, stone and timber from Bristol and to bring luxuries like tobacco and spirits from London. The canal company built the wharf at Pewsey to serve the village, but it was never a great commercial success and was eclipsed by those at nearby Burbage to the east and Honey Street to the west. It remains much as it was in the past. The main buildings consists of a cottage, which would have housed the wharfinger – owner or keeper – of the wharf, and the two-storey warehouse, used to store goods transported by canal.

Facing the canal, turn right along the tow path and walk beside the canal for just over a mile (1.6km) to the second bridge. Cross the stile on your right before the bridge and turn left along the lane, crossing the canal bridge. At a road junction, keep ahead towards downland. Pass cottages on your right and proceed ahead through the gateway along the drive. Where this bears left to **West Wick House**, continue straight on along the grass-centred track,

WHILE YOU'RE THERE

Visit nearby Pewsey and its **heritage centre** in the High Street. Housed in an 1870s foundry, it contains a collection of agricultural machinery. Cut into Pewsey Hill south of the village is the **Pewsey White Horse**, carved in 1937 on the site of an older horse (1785) to celebrate the coronation of George VI. The climb is worth it for the inspiring views.

WHAT TO LOOK FOR ⓘ

From the Giants Grave look west across Oare to locate **Oare House** on the west side of the village. This small mansion has associations with Clough Williams-Ellis of Portmeirion fame. He added the symmetrical wings in the 1920s.

---

which soon narrows and begins to climb steadily towards **Martinsell Hill**. Go through a gate and bear left at the fork to ascend a steep sunken lane (this can be muddy). At the top, keep left of the gate, disregard the waymarked stile on your right and bear left alongside the fence, following a path towards the long barrow on the summit of **Oare Hill**.

The Giants Grave is an ancient unchambered burial site that has a charming legend associated with it. It is claimed that the giant will stir from his slumbers if anyone runs around the tomb seven times. Standing as it does on the top of Oare Hill, it is a splendid vantage point from which to savour far-reaching views across the Vale of Pewsey and the North Wessex Downs. You can also see the impressive combes and dry valleys etched into the downland scarp slopes away to your right. The unimproved chalk downlands along the steep escarpment of the vale and on nearby Martinsell Hill are noted for their extremely rich chalk grassland flora, notably cowslip, burnt orchid and devil's bit scabious, and a wide variety of butterflies including Adonis and chalkhill blue and dark green fritillary butterflies.

Follow the path past the trig point and descend the steep grassy slope towards **Oare**, soon to reach a stile at the bottom. Bear left along the field edge and follow the path across the field to a gate and crossing of ways. Take the footpath ahead, bearing right, then left around the field edge to reach a lane. Cross the stile opposite and bear half-left across the field to a stile. Cut across the field corner to a further stile and turn right along a track. Keep ahead where it bears right towards a farm and continue to the **Kennet and Avon Canal**. Cross the bridge and bear left back down to rejoin the tow path, passing **Jones's Mill – The Vera Jeans Nature Reserve**.

Bordering the River Avon and fed by numerous springs, this wetland reserve, or fen, is a rare environment within Wiltshire and an exciting place because of the diverse wildlife it supports. Since the water-meadows were abandoned, the site has developed an exceptionally rich flora with 14 species of sedge (a grass-like plant) alone. Dotted among the sedge you will also find bogbean, bog pimpernel and southern marsh orchid. An unusual sight are the belted Galloway cattle which graze the fen to keep the coarser vegetation at bay, thus allowing the more delicate flowers to thrive. The wet woodland in the middle of the reserve has an understorey of huge tussock sedges and great horsetails creating a prehistoric landscape. Retrace your steps back to the car park at **Pewsey Wharf**.

WHERE TO EAT AND DRINK ⓘ

Occupying the former wharfinger's cottage and with its small canalside garden, the welcoming **Waterfront Café** at Pewsey Wharf offers light lunches and snacks all day and is the perfect resting place after your walk. Alternatively, try the **French Horn** pub across the bridge.

Walk 11

Salisbury's Historic Trail

A gentle urban stroll around the streets and ancient pathways of one of England's lovliest Cathedral cities.

•DISTANCE•	3 miles (4.8km)
•MINIMUM TIME•	2hrs (longer if visiting attractions)
•ASCENT / GRADIENT•	Negligible
•LEVEL OF DIFFICULTY•	
•PATHS•	Pavements and metalled footpaths
•LANDSCAPE•	City streets and water-meadows
•SUGGESTED MAP•	aqua3 OS Explorer 130 Salisbury & Stonehenge; AA Salisbury streetplan
•START / FINISH•	Grid reference: SU 141303
•DOG FRIENDLINESS•	Not suitable for dogs
•PARKING•	Central car park (signed off A36 Ring Road)
•PUBLIC TOILETS•	Central car park, Market Place, Queen Elizabeth Gardens

BACKGROUND TO THE WALK

Salisbury, or New Sarum, founded in 1220 following the abandonment of Old Sarum and built at the confluence of four rivers, is one of the most beautiful cathedral cities in Britain. Relatively free from the sprawling suburbs and high-rise development common in most cities, the surrounding countryside comes in to meet the city streets along the river valleys. Throughout the city centre, buildings of all styles blend harmoniously, from the 13th-century Bishop's Palace in The Close, the medieval gabled houses and historic inns and market places to stately pedimented Georgian houses and even the modern shopping centre. You will discover a host of architectural treasures on this gentle city stroll.

Majestic Cathedral and Close

Salisbury's skyline is dominated by the magnificent spire of the cathedral, which makes a graceful centrepiece to the unified city. An architectural masterpiece, built in just 38 years during the 13th century, the cathedral is unique for its uniformity of style. The tower and spire, with a combined height of 404ft (123m) – the tallest in England – were added in 1334, and the west front of the building is lavishly decorated with row upon row of beautifully carved statues in niches. The rich and spacious interior contains huge graceful columns of Purbeck stone, which line the high-vaulted nave and many windows add to the airy, dignified interior. You will find the impressive tombs and effigies in the nave, the fine cloisters and the library, home to a copy of the Magna Carta, of particular interest.

Originally built to house the clerics, the Cathedral Close is the one of the largest and finest in Britain. It is entered by a series of medieval gateways and contains several grand structures in a rich variety of architectural styles, dating from the 13th century to the present day. Four of these fine buildings are open to the public as museums. The highlights are probably Malmesbury House, originally a 13th-century canonry, with its magnificent roccoco plasterwork and an Orangery that once sheltered Charles II, and Mompesson House (owned by the National Turst), an exquisite Queen Anne building with period furnishings, china and paintings.

City Streets

Beyond The Close, Salisbury is a delight to explore on foot. You can wander through a fascinating network of medieval streets and alleys, lined with half-timbered and jettied houses, enjoying names like Fish Row, Silver Street and Ox Row. On this city walk you will see St Thomas' Church (1238), noted for its 15th-century Doom painting, believed to be the largest painting of the Last Judgment in existence, and pass the hexagonally buttressed 15th-century Poultry Cross, the last of four market crosses in the city. Note, too, the timbered medieval houses, John A'Port and William Russel's (Watsons china shop) in Queen Street, and the Joiners' Hall with its superb Jacobean façade in St Ann Street.

Away from the hustle and bustle, your riverside stroll through Queen Elizabeth's Gardens and along the Town Path to Harnham Mill will reveal the famous view across the water-meadows to the cathedral, much admired by many an artist.

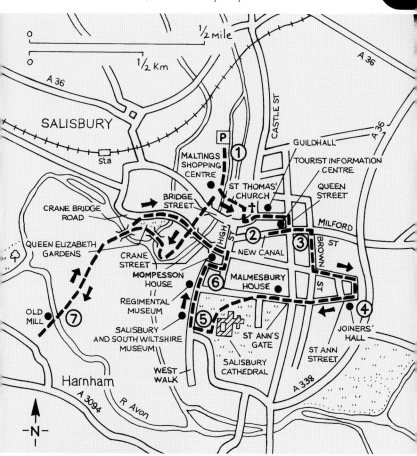

① Join the **Riverside Walk** and follow the path through the **Maltings Shopping Centre**. Keep beside the Avon tributary stream to reach **St Thomas Square**, close to Michael Snell Tea Rooms and St Thomas' Church. Bear right to the junction of **Bridge Street**, **Silver Street** and the **High Street**.

Walk 11

② Turn left along **Silver Street** and cross the pedestrian crossing by the Haunch of Venison pub to the **Poultry Cross**. Keep ahead along **Butcher Row** and **Fish Row** to pass the Guildhall and tourist information centre. Turn right along **Queen Street** and turn right along **New Canal** to view the cinema foyer.

③ Return to the crossroads and continue ahead along **Milford Street** to pass the Red Lion. Turn right along **Brown Street**, then left along **Trinity Street** to pass Trinity Hospital. Pass Love Lane into **Barnard Street** and follow the road right to reach **St Ann Street**, opposite the Joiners' Hall.

> ### WHERE TO EAT AND DRINK
> Old pubs, tea rooms and restaurants abound around the cathedral and its close. Try the excellent **Le Hérisson** café and deli in Crane Street, **Michael Snell Tea Rooms** in St Thomas Square, the historic **Haunch of Venison** in Minster Street, and **Apres LXIX**, a bistro offering modern British food, in New Street. Enjoy a civilised afternoon tea in the garden of **Mompesson House** in The Close.

④ Walk down St Ann Street and keep ahead on merging with Brown Street to reach the T-junction with **St John Street**. Cross straight over and go through St Ann's Gate into the **Cathedral Close**. Pass Malmesbury House and Bishops Walk and take the path diagonally left across the green to reach the main entrance to the cathedral.

> ### WHAT TO LOOK FOR
> Go into the foyer of the cinema in New Canal to view John Halle's 15th-century banqueting hall. Composer George Frideric Handel is thought to have given his first concert in England in the room above St Ann Street Gate. While in the cathedral, look out for the 14th-century clock, believed to be the oldest working clock in the world.

⑤ Pass the entrance, walk beside the barrier ahead and turn right. Shortly, turn right again along **West Walk**, passing Salisbury and South Wiltshire Museum, Discover Salisbury (in the Medieval Hall), and the Regimental Museum. Keep ahead into **Chorister Green** to pass Mompesson House.

⑥ Bear left through the gates into **High Street** and turn left at the crossroads along **Crane Street**. Cross the River Avon and turn left along the metalled path beside the river through **Queen Elizabeth Gardens**. Keep left by the play area and soon cross the footbridge to follow the **Town Path** across the water-meadows to the **Old Mill** (hotel) in Harnham.

⑦ Return along Town Path, cross the footbridge and keep ahead to **Crane Bridge Road**. Turn right, recross the Avon and turn immediately left along the riverside path to **Bridge Street**. Cross straight over and follow the path ahead towards **Bishops Mill**. Walk back through the **Maltings Shopping Centre** to the car park.

> ### WHILE YOU'RE THERE
> Discover more about Salisbury's fascinating history by visiting the award-winning **Salisbury and South Wiltshire Museum**, housed in the 14th-century King's House within The Close. In the Medieval Hall, also in The Close, **Discover Salisbury** offers a big screen presentation of the city's history and attractions. Climb the steps up the cathedral tower for a bird's-eye view across the city and surrounding countryside.

Lydiard Park – Swindon's Surprise

A gentle rural ramble from a Palladian mansion and country park on Swindon's urban fringe.

•DISTANCE•	3¼ miles (5.3km)
•MINIMUM TIME•	2hrs
•ASCENT / GRADIENT•	65ft (20m) ▲ ▲ ▲
•LEVEL OF DIFFICULTY•	🚶 🚶 🚶
•PATHS•	Field paths (can be muddy), tracks and metalled lanes, 11 stiles
•LANDSCAPE•	Farmland, parkland, woodland
•SUGGESTED MAP•	aqua3 OS Explorer 169 Cirencester & Swindon
•START / FINISH•	Grid reference: SU 101844
•DOG FRIENDLINESS•	Can be off lead in country park
•PARKING•	Free parking at Lydiard Country Park
•PUBLIC TOILETS•	Lydiard Country Park

BACKGROUND TO THE WALK

Right on the edge of the modern town of Swindon lies the 244 acre (99ha) Lydiard Park, an easily accessible and delightful buffer against any further westward urban spread. Within the wooded and eminently explorable park is one of Wiltshire's smaller and lesser known stately homes, a Palladian mansion, the ancestral home of the Viscounts Bolingbroke and their church, St Mary's, in the village of Lydiard Tregoze. This walk takes you through the park and across farmland following rights of way and Swindon's new Millennium Trail.

Lydiard House and Park

The present house, built in 1743, was saved from dereliction by the Swindon Corporation in 1943. Part of the property now serves as a hostel but the ground floor has been restored to its former 19th-century glory, complete with ornate plasterwork, original family furnishings, a rare painted glass window, portraits of the St John family (the Bolingbrokes) who lived here from Elizabethan times and lifelike waxwork inhabitants. As one of Wiltshire's smaller stately homes, it has an intimate atmosphere rarely found in larger houses which have opened their doors to the public. Here you have the impression of stepping back in time to pay a social call on wealthy relations, a family, which like many of us, has had its share of ups and downs. Even the park has had its misfortunes; it was used as a prisoner of war camp at the end of the Second World War and lost all the fine elm trees, which lined the driveway from 1911, to Dutch elm disease.

The Bolingbroke Family

During the Civil War the Bolingbroke's sided with the losing Royalists and although rewarded during the Restoration were disappointed when Henry St John (1652–1742) was bestowed with the title of a 'mere' Viscount in 1712 rather than becoming an Earl. Rather too close a friendship with France in the early 18th century led to a period of exile for Henry before he received a royal pardon. In 1768 the Second Viscount, Frederick St John, sensationally for the time, divorced his wife, Lady Diana Spencer, daughter of the Duke of Marlborough. Further periods of 'absenteeism', this time to Germany and heavy mortgage liabilities finally saw the break up of the estate in the 1920s and 30s.

St Mary's Church

The church contains a further history of the family in the form of memorials. Family trees, paintings, stained-glass windows and tomb effigies are all in evidence. The most impressive of the latter is The Golden Cavalier, a magnificent, lifesize, fully gilded, statue of Sir John St John (1585–1648). He emerges from his tent fully clad for one of the Civil War battles. As imposing as he looks one cannot but think of the inner sadness of a man who in that conflict lost his King and three of his sons.

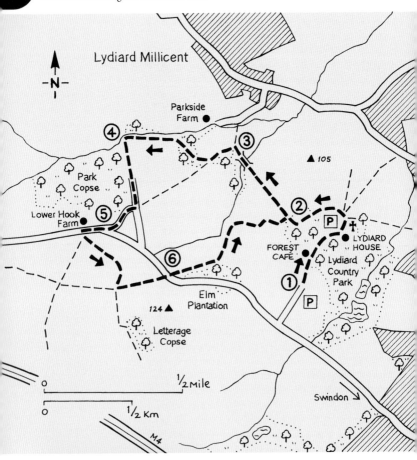

Walk 12 Directions

① Turn left out of the car park, pass the **Forest Café** and a wooden barrier and continue along the track

to **Lydiard House** and the church. At the church, bear left through the car park, ignoring the stile on your right, and go through a gate. Walk beside a walled garden and follow the path left into woodland.

WHAT TO LOOK FOR ℹ

Look out for the **ice house**, which supplied ice to the Lydiard kitchens, and the 18th-century **Ha Ha**, a steep-sided brick-lined trench which kept cattle and sheep out of the park. In **St Mary's Church** look for the 15th-century wall paintings and the splendid 17th-century St John Triptych, a monument of painted display panels commemorating the St John family.

② Just before reaching a small clearing, turn right (it's marked by a red striped post) to reach a kissing gate and cattle grid on the woodland edge. Proceed straight ahead across the field on a defined path to a stile and plank bridge in the right-hand corner.

③ Continue through the edge of a small plantation, passing beneath electricity cables, and turn left across a stile in the corner of the plantation. Follow the waymarker across the field to a stile and turn right, following the path within the edge of woodland. Bear left, then right, climb wooden steps and, emerging in the corner of a field, turn left with the red striped post marker and cross a stile.

④ Go across the gap (can be muddy) between two fields to a waymarker, then follow the right-hand field edge to a stile and gate.

WHILE YOU'RE THERE ℹ

Near by, in Swindon, you'll find **Steam – Museum of the Great Western Railway**, where you will discover the remarkable story of the railway by means of various imaginative and fascinating exhibits. At Blunsdon Station, near Purton, is the **Swindon and Cricklade Railway**, Wiltshire's only standard gauge heritage railway which operates both steam and diesel locomotives.

Follow the farm track ahead, then just beyond the first of two metal barriers, turn right down the track to the road.

⑤ Turn right then, in about 200yds (183m), take the arrowed footpath to the left through a gate. Bear half-left to double stiles and maintain your direction to a further stile. Turn sharp right along the field edge to reach a gate by a barn, then bear half-left across the field, passing beneath electricity power cables to a stile in the corner.

WHERE TO EAT AND DRINK ℹ

Seek refreshment in the **Forest Café** within the park's visitor centre, or head further afield to the **Three Crowns** at Brinkworth (west off B4042) for excellent pub food. Alternatively, picnic beneath shady trees on the lawn in front of Lydiard House.

⑥ Cut diagonally across the road to a stile and gate. Bear right around the field edge, alongside a small copse to a stile. Almost immediately turn left through a gate and walk down a long narrow field. Swing right with the field boundary and eventually turn right across the stile by the cattle grid encountered on your outward route. Retrace your steps back to the country park and car park.

Grovely Wood from Great Wishford

Learn all about Wiltshire's oldest surviving custom on this peaceful walk through ancient Grovely Wood.

•DISTANCE•	5 miles (8km)
•MINIMUM TIME•	2hrs 30min
•ASCENT / GRADIENT•	370ft (113m) ▲▲▲
•LEVEL OF DIFFICULTY•	🚶🚶 🚶 🚶
•PATHS•	Woodland paths and downland tracks
•LANDSCAPE•	Chalk downland, wooded hillside and lush water-meadow
•SUGGESTED MAP•	aqua3 OS Explorer 130 Salisbury & Stonehenge
•START / FINISH•	Grid reference: SU 080353
•DOG FRIENDLINESS•	Can be off lead through Grovely Wood
•PARKING•	Roadside parking in South Street, Great Wishford
•PUBLIC TOILETS•	None on route

BACKGROUND TO THE WALK

Great Wishford is the most southerly of a delightful series of villages that nestle in the valley of the River Wylye, which gives its name to Wilton and therefore also to the county of Wiltshire. Our knowledge of the village pre-dates the Norman conquest in 1066, the written name changing over the years from Wicheford or Witford to Willesford Magna in the mid-16th century and by the early 17th century it was known as Wishford Magna. Many of the village houses are constructed of Chilmark stone, quarried over the hill in the next valley. Some are interlaced with flint, others are thatched and many are steeply roofed and date from 1628.

'Grovely and All Grovely'

Mention the village of Great Wishford and most Wiltshire people will immediately associate it with one date in the calendar – 29th May. This is Oak Apple Day, when the only ancient custom still taking place in the county is enacted by the villagers. On this day they commemorate their victory over the local landowner, the Earl of Pembroke, who in creating Wilton Park closed the east–west road, south of the River Nadder, thus interfering with their ancient rights – from a charter granted in 1603 – to cut and gather timber in the nearby Grovely Wood.

Celebrations begin at dawn when the young people of the village wake each household in turn by banging tin pans and shouting 'Grovely, Grovely, Grovely and All Grovely'. Armed with billhooks and accompanied by traditional musicians they walk up Grovely Lane into the woods, where they cut green branches for their houses and an oak bough which is decked with ribbons and hung from the church tower. Villagers dressed in period costume and led by the parish rector then go on to Salisbury Cathedral where further celebrations, in the form of dancing on the cathedral green and a procession to the high altar, culminate in the villagers loudly proclaiming their rights and chanting 'Grovely! Grovely! and All Grovely! Unity is strength'.

Midsummer Tithes Auction

These unusual village celebrations are not a merely modern revival of a long-lost tradition but actually seem to date back to a pagan and primitive period when tree worship was connected with May Day celebrations. In understanding how these ancient rights, customs and traditions have survived in Great Wishford it is interesting to note that the village has been in the ownership of just three families over the last seven centuries.

Bread Stones

An unusual feature in the village are the stone inscriptions that can be found in the east wall of the churchyard. These tablets record the price of bread in the village since the Napoleonic Wars. In 1801 is was 3s 10d a gallon, in 1904 only 10d and by 1920 it had risen to 2s 8d. The 'Gall' measures are a reminder of the days when bread was sold in semi-liquid form as dough for home baking.

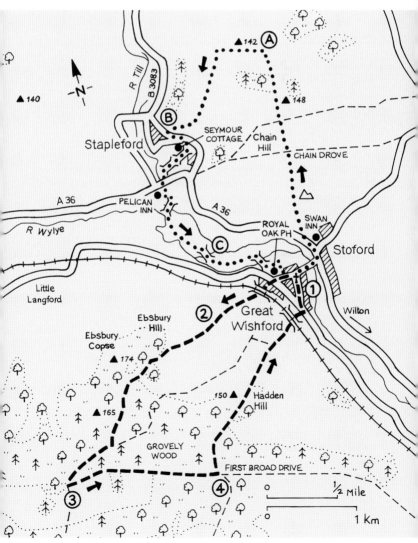

Walk 13 Directions

① Return along **South Street** to the church and turn left at the T-junction. Walk past the **Royal Oak**. Go under the railway bridge and immediately turn right along the waymarked bridle path beside a cemetery. Ascend the track to a gate.

② Walk along the left-hand field edge to a gate, then bear right around the top of the field making for the gate that leads into woodland. Turn immediately left along the woodland track. Turn left at the next T-junction and walk down the well-defined track (permissive bridle path) to another T-junction. Turn right up the metalled lane.

③ At a major junction, turn sharp left on to a gravel track. Follow it left, pass beside a metal barrier and join a metalled track running down a broad beech avenue (**First Broad Drive**) along the course of a Roman road, or Lead Road, which traversed Wessex from the lead mines of the Mendips in Somerset to join other

ancient routes at Old Sarum, such as the Harrow Way to Kent. You are now walking through **Grovely Wood**, a fine stretch of woodland that was once a royal hunting forest and which, together with the New Forest and Cranborne Chase, formed a very significant preserve.

WHAT TO LOOK FOR ⓘ

Spend time in the **Church of St Giles** in Great Wishford. Note the tombs of two old village families the Bonhams and Grobhams, and the parish fire engine, one of the earliest fire engines ever built. Made entirely of wood by Richard Newsham in 1728, it could provide 65 gallons (295 litres) of water and cost the churchwardens £33 3s 0d. Surprisingly, it was last used as recently as 1970 to fight a blaze in the village.

---

④ After a mile (1.6km), at a crossing of public bridle paths, turn left and keep to the main track downhill through the woodland, ignoring all cross paths and forks. Emerge from **Grovely Wood** and follow the track downhill towards **Great Wishford**. Pass beneath the railway line to the lane. Turn left, then fork right along **South Street**.

WHERE TO EAT AND DRINK ⓘ

Local ales and traditional pub meals, including a Sunday carvery, are served in the creeper-clad **Royal Oak** in Great Wishford, the ideal refuelling place if you're on Walk 14. Alternatively, try the **Swan Inn** at Stoford or the **Pelican Inn** at Stapleford, both offer pub food and have riverside gardens.

WHILE YOU'RE THERE ⓘ

Nearby **Wilton**, the former capital of Saxon Wessex, offers plenty of interest. Wilton House, home to the Earls of Pembroke, is a splendid 17th-century mansion boasting a famous art collection, fine furniture and 21 acres (8.5ha) of landscaped parkland. Take a tour around the Wilton Carpet Factory and learn about carpet making based on 300 years of tradition. Explore the town's museum and, if time allows, visit the impressive Italian-style Church of St Mary and St Nicholas.

Till and Wylye Valleys

An optional loop to Stapleford via downland droves and riverside paths.
See map and information panel for Walk 13

Walk 14

•DISTANCE•	5 miles (8km)
•MINIMUM TIME•	2hrs 30min
•ASCENT / GRADIENT•	278ft (85m) ▲▲▲
•LEVEL OF DIFFICULTY•	🚶 🚶 🚶

Walk 14 Directions (Walk 13 option)

Unlike many of the chalk downland valleys across the Salisbury Plain, the valley of the River Till is the only one with a permanent flow of water. Numerous springs high up in the heart of the plain continuously feed the little river, which rises near Tilshead and flows south to merge with the much larger River Wylye at Stapleford.

Walk to the T-junction by the church and turn right along **West Street**, crossing the river to the A36. Turn left, cross the road just past the pub and fork right uphill along a track. Climb through trees and continue between fields. Keep straight on over **Chain Drove**, by a barn, and the next crossing of byways. Pass a copse and soon take the track left, Point Ⓐ. Follow this track as it bears sharp left, then heads downhill and veers right, eventually reaching a lane in **Stapleford**, Point Ⓑ.

There are seven other Staplefords in England, for Stapleford is the name given by the Saxons to a common feature of 'a ford marked by a post or staple' which would probably serve to indicate the shallowest place in the stream. In Wiltshire it became the name of a strategic point where the ancient road from Old Sarum to Bath crosses the Till. There are four distinct parts of the village – Uppington, Church Street, Overstreet (or 'the settlement opposite') which lies clustered beside a castle mound dating from the 12th century, and Serrington beside the A36.

Turn left, then cross the B3083 on to a bridle path. Turn left along a fenced path at **Seymour Cottage**, cross two footbridges and soon go through a gate to the A36. Cross over, turn right, then left along the footpath before the bridge. Cross a stile, follow the right-hand field edge to a stile and plank bridges, then cross a field towards a stile near a willow. Before the stile, turn left alongside the **River Wylye** to a stile and footbridge, Point Ⓒ.

Keep the river to your right, crossing more stiles and footbridges. In 100yds (91m) beyond a thatched cottage, climb the stile on your right, then cross a footbridge and further stile before turning left towards farm buildings. Cross a stile and turn right up the drive to the lane and turn left back to the church and **South Street**.

Sarsen Stones on Fyfield Down

Explore a prehistoric landscape on this fascinating downland ramble.

•DISTANCE•	6 miles (9.7km)
•MINIMUM TIME•	2hrs 30min
•ASCENT / GRADIENT•	328ft (100m) ▲▲▲
•LEVEL OF DIFFICULTY•	👫 👫 👫
•PATHS•	Downland tracks and field paths
•LANDSCAPE•	Lofty downland pasture and gallops
•SUGGESTED MAP•	aqua3 OS Explorer 157 Marlborough & Savernake Forest
•START / FINISH•	Grid reference: SU 159699
•DOG FRIENDLINESS•	Can be off lead along Ridgeway path
•PARKING•	Car park close to Manton House Estate (right off A4, signed Manton, west of Marlborough)
•PUBLIC TOILETS•	None on route

Walk 15 Directions

Leave the car park by the track in the top right-hand corner, signposted '**White Horse Trail to Avebury and Hackpen**'. Follow the track right and shortly fork left, continuing between high hedges (private roads right), then on between the gallops across **Clatford Down** with good views. On reaching a T-junction by a covered reservoir, turn left along the **Herepath** (Green Street).

The Herepath is an ancient east–west route across the Marlborough Downs. The name is

derived from the Old English word 'here' meaning an army or multitude. It suggests that this may have been one of the defensive routes established by King Alfred in the 9th century in his struggle with the Danes.

Shortly, turn right through a gate waymarked '**Hackpen**', to join a grassy track alongside a conifer plantation, then head across pasture to a gate into woodland. Follow the track (can be muddy) through the sparse woodland then, on leaving the wood, keep straight on along the right-hand field edge. Turn left down a track in the field corner. Pass a gate on the right and continue between fields to reach the **Ridgeway**. This ancient highway incorporates a complicated network of green lanes, and follows a natural route on high ground. It was used as a drove road or trading route and a convenient means for invaders, peaceful or war-like, to penetrate the heartland of southern England

---

WHERE TO EAT AND DRINK ℹ️
There are no refreshment places along the route but, if you bring your own. the Ridgeway track with its far-reaching views provides the perfect picnic spot. Nearby Manton and Lockeridge have pubs, while Marlborough offers the full range of refreshment facilities.

before Anglo-Saxon times. The Ridgeway National Trail forms only part of the route, although by linking several trails you can walk the entire route.

Turn left along the rutted and often muddy track for ¾ mile (1.2km) then, at the crossways by an information board, turn left through a gate on to **Fyfield Down**.

A feature of Fyfield Down and neighbouring Overton Down are the sarsen stones that litter this intriguing chalk limestone landscape. Sarsens are natural deposits of extremely hard siliceous sandstone that derive from Tertiary deposits, later eroded and moved by glaciation some 25 million years ago. Although found elsewhere, they are not on the scale seen in the Marlborough district. Sarsens are also known as 'druid stones' or 'grey wethers', the latter due to their resemblance at a distance to a flock of sheep, the word 'wether' coming from the Old English for sheep.

Sarsens have been of great importance to humans since prehistoric times. The hard flints were used to make hand axes and other useful tools during the Bronze Age. From the 5th century to the mid-19th century, sarsens were used for building stone, constructing the nearby villages of West Overton and Lockeridge, gateposts, and as paving stones and tramway setts. More importantly, Fyfield Down was the stone quarry supplying Avebury stone circle and possibly Stonehenge. Stones weighing as much as 40 tons were dug up, sometimes shaped, and dragged over the downs by hundreds of people pulling them on wooden rollers with woven grass ropes.

In 1956 Fyfield Down was declared a National Nature Reserve, not only to protect this fine stretch of natural downland and Britain's best assemblage of sarsen stones, which support nationally important lichens, but also to preserve the extensive prehistoric field systems that exist here. As you stride across this rock-strewn landscape, note the chequerboard appearance of the field systems. Banks or 'lynchets' some 8ft (3m) high have formed where sarsens had been moved to create field boundaries, arresting soil movement caused by ploughing over the centuries.

WHILE YOU'RE THERE
Visit **Avebury** (▶ Walks 18 and 19) to view the largest stone circle in Europe and explore the Alexander Keiller Museum to learn more about the prehistoric archaeology of this area.

Proceed along a grassy track and cross a gallop via three gates. This is prime racehorse training country and there are many racing stables in the area. Continue to the right of a wood, then in the valley bottom, fork right off the gravel track and ascend a grassy track, passing more sarsen stones. At the top, go through the two gates that cut the corner of a wooded enclosure and turn right along the field edge, ignoring the stile on the right. Pass through a gate in the bottom corner, cross a gallop and continue straight on across grassland on a defined path. Cross another gallop, then follow the path right over a further gallop to a furlong pole at the end of a line of trees. Swing left over yet more gallops to a waymarker post, then turn left to cross two more gallops to reach a gate. Turn right and follow the outward route back to the car park.

Walk 16

Old Sarum

Explore the Avon Valley and fortified Old Sarum.

•DISTANCE•	6 miles (9.7km)
•MINIMUM TIME•	2hrs
•ASCENT / GRADIENT•	557ft (170m) ▲▲▲
•LEVEL OF DIFFICULTY•	🚶 🚶 🚶
•PATHS•	Footpaths, tracks, bridle paths, stretches of road, 12 stiles
•LANDSCAPE•	Downland, river valley, castle rampart
•SUGGESTED MAP•	aqua3 OS Explorer 130 Salisbury & Stonehenge
•START / FINISH•	Grid reference: SU 139326
•DOG FRIENDLINESS•	Keep dogs on leads at all times
•PARKING•	English Heritage car park (closes 6PM; 4PM winter)
•PUBLIC TOILETS•	Old Sarum car park

BACKGROUND TO THE WALK

Set on a bleak hill overlooking modern-day Salisbury (New Sarum) stand the massive, deserted ramparts and earthworks of the original settlement of Old Sarum. People have lived on this windswept hilltop for some 5,000 years, the outer banks and ditches were constructed during the Iron Age to create a huge hill fort. It was later inhabited by the Romans and several Roman roads converge on the site. The Saxons followed and developed a town within the prehistoric ramparts.

The Rise of Christianity

Soon after the Conquest, the Norman invaders realised the camp's strength and built the inner earthworks by 1070. Within the massive hilltop defences they built a royal castle, two palaces, and in 1075, Bishop Osmund constructed the first cathedral. The imposition of Norman rule had a profound effect on English society, in particular upon the Church, remodelling its structure, giving a new impetus to the building or reconstruction of parish churches and encouraging the development of new monasteries and other religious institutions. This is no more evident than at Old Sarum.

Osmund's cathedral set new standards which were widely adopted in other English cathedrals. Instead of being run on monastic lines, it was served by 36 canons living in separate lodgings under the direction of four officers. The architecture was Romanesque and characterised by its lavish scale. Following Osmund's death in 1099, Bishop Roger was responsible for the ambitious rebuilding of the cathedral soon after 1100.

Old Sarum rapidly developed and for 150 years it was a thriving medieval city due to its position at a major crossroads and its central location in southern England. As the cathedral grew more powerful, it was obvious that friction would develop between the clergy and the military governor of the castle at Old Sarum. After Roger's death in 1139, the city went into decline and quarrelling increased between the two powers. The vitality and wealth of the Church, combined with the exposed site, lack of space to expand the cathedral and the shortage of water at Old Sarum, led to the removal of the cathedral to a new city by the River Avon in the early 13th century. Building work on the new cathedral began in 1220 and was largely completed by 1250.

The castle remained in use until Tudor times and was one of the most notorious rotten boroughs in the country when in 1832, only ten voters returned two Members of Parliament; one was William Pitt the Elder, Prime Minister from 1766 to 1768. Today, it is deserted and you can roam across the 56 acres (22ha) of ramparts and ruins, admiring the Avon Valley views with the spire of Salisbury Cathedral, at 404ft (123m) England's highest spire, dominating the skyline. A fee is charged to view the inner bailey ruins.

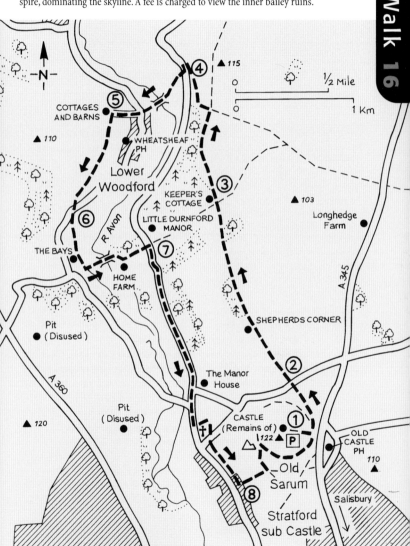

Walk 16 **Directions**

① From the car park walk down the access road through the outer bank of the fortified site. Ignore the

gates on your left, which provide access to the upper and lower ramparts. Go through the two gates leading to a waymarked and fenced bridle path and follow this until you reach a road.

Walk 16

② Go through the gate opposite and follow the track ahead. Pass a cottage (**Shepherds Corner**) and ascend the track. In ¼ mile (400m), descend to **Keeper's Cottage** and a crossing of paths.

③ Keep straight on, heading uphill and between fields into a wooded area. At a crossing of bridle paths, turn left and descend a tree-lined path. At a boundary marker, bear right and continue to a road.

WHAT TO LOOK FOR

Just south of Old Sarum, on a hedged bridle path, is the site of the **Parliament Tree**. A commemoration stone, erected in 1931, marks the spot where William Pitt the Elder, the 18th-century Prime Minister, and another MP were elected when only ten voters returned them to Parliament. This act made Old Sarum one of the 'rotten boroughs' that were abolished by the Reform Act of 1832.

④ Turn left, then in 50yds (46m), turn right down a metalled lane (cul-de-sac). Cross the **River Avon** and two further footbridges, then follow the metalled path and drive to a road. For the **Wheatsheaf** turn left. Turn right and in 50yds (46m), turn left up a lane.

⑤ Just before cottages and barns, turn left over a stile and walk down the left-hand field edge, crossing two more stiles and fields. Maintain direction across the next field, cross a track and go through the hedge ahead, then in 100yds (91m) reach a stile and road.

⑥ Cross the road diagonally and take the path down a wooded track. Pass to the left of 'The Bays' to a stile and turn right between the stream and fence. Cross double stiles in the corner and turn sharp left over a stile and turn right beside the stream to a white gate and a metalled drive. Turn left and skirt **Home Farm** and **Little Durnford Manor** to a gate and road.

⑦ Turn right and follow the road for ¾ mile (1.2km) to a staggered crossroads. Keep ahead towards **Stratford sub Castle**, crossing the stile on your left in 100yds (91m). Follow the right-hand field edge around the churchyard, cross a stile, a metalled path and a further stile and bear half-right to a gate in the field corner. Head down the next field, pass a barn and cross a stile on to a fenced track.

⑧ Turn left uphill towards the tree-covered ramparts. Keep left at the junction of paths by a gate, then shortly fork right and steeply climb on to the outer rampart. Turn right and follow the path to a gate and Old Sarum's access road. Turn left back to the car park.

WHERE TO EAT AND DRINK

Opposite the main entrance to the car park to Old Sarum is the **Old Castle** which offers traditional pub food, children's facilities and a spacious garden. The **Wheatsheaf** (halfway through the walk) offers good food and a riverside garden. The entrance kiosk/shop to the Inner Bailey has a tea/coffee machine.

WHILE YOU'RE THERE

Savour the picturesque drive north through the Avon Valley and the Woodford villages. Stop off at **Heale Gardens** (open all year), an 8 acre (3.2ha) riverside garden noted for its great drifts of snowdrops, early spring colours, varied collections of plants, shrubs and roses growing in a formal setting of clipped hedges, and its magnificent water garden with magnolias and an authentic Japanese Tea House.

Pewsey Vale and Down

A varied ramble across chalk downland, rich in archaeological and natural treasures, and beside the Kennet and Avon Canal in the fertile Vale of Pewsey.

•DISTANCE•	7 miles (11.6km)
•MINIMUM TIME•	3hrs
•ASCENT / GRADIENT•	492ft (150m) ▲▲▲
•LEVEL OF DIFFICULTY•	🚶🚶 🚶🚶 🚶
•PATHS•	Tracks, field paths, tow path, metalled lanes, 4 stiles
•LANDSCAPE•	High downland pasture, Vale of Pewsey, village streets
•SUGGESTED MAP•	aqua3 OS Explorer 157 Marlborough & Savernake Forest
•START / FINISH•	Grid reference: SU 115637
•DOG FRIENDLINESS•	Keep dogs under control across downland pasture
•PARKING•	Tan Hill car park
•PUBLIC TOILETS•	None on route

BACKGROUND TO THE WALK

No one who travels in Wiltshire can fail to be impressed by the sweep of softly rounded chalk downland that rises to over 800ft (244m) above the fertile farmlands of the Vale of Pewsey. Walking across such high ground is one of the greatest walking experiences in the county. Not only are the views some of the best in Wiltshire, the land is rich in ancient settlements, frontier lines and burial sites. This walk is varied and exhilarating, encapsulating these archaeological treasures as well as exploring the vale with its meandering canal and unspoilt villages. It is a tale of travelling and travellers, a pre-occupation we have had since the dawn of time, travelling for sustenance, for conquest, for trade and for pleasure.

Walking Wansdyke

The high and relatively unforested downland ridges were the pre-historic motorways. They also became the boundaries between clans and kingdoms. For the defence of one in post-Roman times, the massive bank and ditch of the Wansdyke was built, clearly visible for 12 miles (19.3km) in Wiltshire from Morgan Hill to Savernake Forest. At least two major Saxon battles were fought along its length, one in AD 592 by the neolithic long barrow now known as Adam's Grave, the best sited long barrow in Wiltshire. In more peaceful times the Wansdyke became a natural road for drovers bringing their animals to the great stock fairs at Tan Hill, echoing not only the tramp of herdsmen, but the cows and sheep that were often shod for the long trek.

Saxon settlers would have been attracted by the springs and pastureland in the valley and villages would have been established, although the twin villages of Alton Barnes and Alton Priors seem scarcely large enough to make one village. Nonetheless, each had its own church, linked by an interesting sarsen stone footpath. Next upon the scene were the navvies and bargees when the Kennet and Avon Canal was built between 1794 and 1810, providing an important link between Bristol and London. Unfortunately for the canal and its total of 107 locks, the benefits were short lived when Brunel's railway from London to Bristol opened in 1841.

Alton Barnes White Horse

Spiritual as well as physical journeys also figure in this landscape. High on the downs in tumuli and barrows lie ancient chieftains, with our nearer ancestors in homely churchyards. Wiltshire is famous for the chalk figures in honour of the horse, our long-valued travelling companion. However the one etched into Milk Hill above Alton Barnes is relatively recent. Created in 1812, it measures 166ft (50m) high by 160ft (49m) long and is noted for the fact that the journeyman artist absconded with the £20 fee before completing the task. He was subsequently caught and hung for his crime! No perpetrators have yet suffered that fate for the crop circles, which now regularly decorate the great sweeping fields of corn around Alton Barnes. Hints of yet further journeys to come?

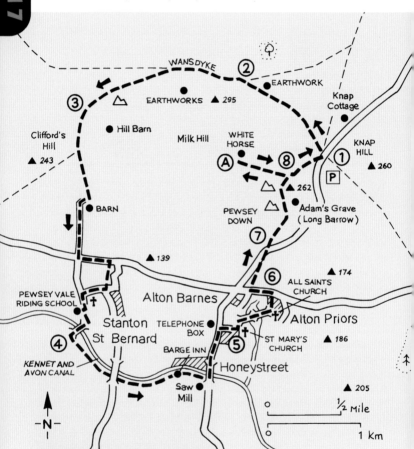

Walk 17 **Directions**

① From the car park, cross the road to a gate and follow the grassy track along the left-hand field edge to a stile and gate. Ascend to further stile and gate, continue uphill and soon descend through earthworks to a T-junction with the **Wansdyke**.

② Turn left and continue with earthworks on your left. Begin to descend, cross a wooden barrier, then go through a gate and bear left off the Wansdyke on to a metalled

Walk 17

track. Just after the track becomes concrete, fork right through a gate and follow the grassy track downhill to a stile and gate.

③ Rejoin the main track by a barn. Pass more barns and continue down to the road. Turn left and take the footpath right just before the turning for Stanton St Bernard. The footpath becomes a metalled lane. At the T-junction, turn right and pass the church, then swing right to **Pewsey Vale Riding School**. Turn left here and follow the track to the **Kennet and Avon Canal**.

④ Cross the canal and bear left through a gate to join the tow path. Keep to the tow path for 1 mile (1.6km), passing the **Barge Inn**, and bear left up to the road at **Honeystreet**. Turn left over the bridge into **Alton Barnes**. In 100yds (91m) past the telephone box, turn right, signed to **St Mary's Church**.

⑤ Just before the church, turn left through a turnstile and walk down a cobbled path. Follow the path

right, cross two footbridges via turnstiles then, where the path turns sharp right to **All Saints Church** in Alton Priors, turn sharp left across the field to a kissing gate and a road.

⑥ Turn left then, just beyond the village sign, take the footpath right up the right-hand field edge. At a kink in the field boundary, follow the waymarker left across the field towards a white sign beyond the boundary. At the road, ascend and fork left up a track to a gate leading on to **Pewsey Down**.

⑦ Follow the waymarker steeply uphill. The path swings left around the hillside, then right up a small valley. Here you can take the path left to the **White Horse**, Point Ⓐ.

⑧ Continue over the hill, then bear right down a combe towards the road. Before reaching the road, bear left over a wooden barrier and follow the right-hand field edge to a stile. Turn right through the gate and cross the road to the car park

Avebury – Pagan Pastures

Explore the famous stone circle and some fine prehistoric monuments.

•**DISTANCE**•	5 miles (8km)
•**MINIMUM TIME**•	2hrs 30min
•**ASCENT / GRADIENT**•	262ft (80m)
•**LEVEL OF DIFFICULTY**•	
•**PATHS**•	Tracks, field paths, some road walking, 3 stiles
•**LANDSCAPE**•	Downland pasture, water-meadows, woodland and village
•**SUGGESTED MAP**•	aqua3 OS Explorer 157 Marlborough & Savernake Forest
•**START / FINISH**•	Grid reference: SU 099696
•**DOG FRIENDLINESS**•	Keep dogs under control across pasture and NT property
•**PARKING**•	Large National Trust car park in Avebury
•**PUBLIC TOILETS**•	Avebury

BACKGROUND TO THE WALK

Avebury's great stone circle is one of the most important megalithic monuments in Europe and it shares it setting with a pretty village. The 200 stones (only 27 remain) were enclosed in a massive earthen rampart nearly a mile (1.6km) in circumference. One can only wonder at the skill, vision and beliefs, not to mention the sheer dogged hard work, which enabled the peoples of that time to move huge stones for many miles and dig thousands of tons of earth to create such landscapes.

Alexander Keiller's Vision

The views presented to today's visitor to Avebury owe as much to archaeologist Alexander Keiller as to the vision of our ancient ancestors. Keiller was the heir to a fortune made from marmalade and was able to indulge in his passion for archaeology. In the early 1930s he came to Avebury, which then had a thriving community within and around the 4,500-year-old circle, and determined to restore it to how it must have looked originally; a prehistoric complex on a scale to match any in the country.

All his energies and a large part of his fortune was spent on purchasing the land, excavating the stones, and although contentious to modern archaeologists, he re-erected fallen stones and set up concrete markers to replace those he believed were missing. Trees were cleared from the ditches and, as and when the opportunity arose, buildings within the circle were purchased and demolished. Some of the villagers left the area and others went to the new houses in nearby Avebury Truslow.

Keiller's work was curtailed by lack of funds and, after the Second World War, he sold the site to the National Trust. His full dreams were never realised and questions were raised as to whether he should have tried to restore the site. Should ancient landscapes be protected by riding roughshod over the interests of those who have subsequently come to live and work there? Whatever your views, there is much to see and enjoy on this walk.

Walking around Avebury is a memorable experience. Unlike Stonehenge, you can roam freely here and this enthralling walk lets you explore some of Britain's finest prehistoric monuments. There is an imposing 1½ mile (2.4km) avenue of standing stones from where, perhaps, ancient processions would lead down to Silbury Hill, an entirely artificial structure

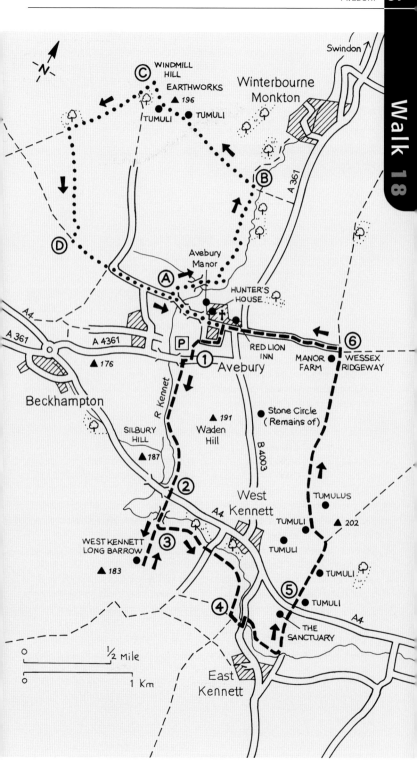

130ft (40m) high. Smaller in scale but just as thought provoking is the West Kennett Long Barrow, the second largest barrow in Britain at 300ft (91m) in length, and there is a liberal scattering of tumuli over the entire area, the last resting places of many a noble and priest. Finally, alongside the A4 and doubtless unnoticed by many motorists, is The Sanctuary, the site of major wooden buildings, possibly used for religious and burial rites. Or did they, like us, take pleasure from seeking views across our wonderful countryside?

Walk 18 **Directions**

① From the car park, walk back to the main road and turn right. In 50yds (46m), cross and go through a gate, signed '**West Kennett Long Barrow**'. Pass through another gate and follow the path alongside the **River Kennet**. Go through two more gates and cross two stiles, your route passing **Silbury Hill**.

② Beyond a gate, walk down the right-hand field edge to a gate and the **A4**. Cross straight over and turn left, then almost immediately right through a gate. Walk down the gravel track and cross a bridge over a stream, the track soon narrowing to a footpath. Go through a kissing gate and turn sharp left.

③ To visit **West Kennett Long Barrow** shortly turn right. Otherwise go straight on around the left-hand field edge to a gate and continue along a track. At a staggered junction, keep ahead across a stile and walk along the right-hand field boundary. Keep right in the corner by a redundant stile and cross the stile on your right in the next corner and proceed up a narrow footpath.

④ At a T-junction, turn left and descend to the road. Turn left, then just beyond the bridge, take the bridle path sharp right. Follow the right-hand field edge to a gap in the corner and keep left through the next field. At the top you'll see tumuli right and **The Sanctuary** left. Continue to the **A4**.

> **WHILE YOU'RE THERE**
> To learn more about Keiller, visit the **Alexander Keiller Museum** which displays many of the exciting finds from his archaeological excavations on Windmill Hill, Silbury Hill, West Kennet Long Barrow and, of course, Avebury.

⑤ Cross the **A4** and head up the **Ridgeway**. After 500yds (457m), turn left off the Ridgeway on to a byway. Bear half-right by the clump of trees on a tumuli and keep to the established track, eventually reaching a T-junction by a series of farm buildings, **Manor Farm**.

⑥ Turn left, signed '**Avebury**', and follow the metalled track through the earthwork and straight over the staggered crossroads by the **Red Lion Inn**. Turn left opposite the National Trust signpost and walk back to the car park.

> **WHAT TO LOOK FOR**
> Wander freely around the **stone circles**, locate the huge Druid Stone, the Swindon Stone and the Barber Stone, and marvel at how they were transported and why they stay upright.

> **WHERE TO EAT AND DRINK**
> Try the thatched **Red Lion** in the heart of the stone circle for traditional pub food and atmosphere. Good home-made vegetarian, mostly organic food and cream teas can be enjoyed at the **Circle Restaurant** off the High Street.

Avebury and Windmill Hill

A slightly shorter loop to the largest neolithic enclosure in Britain.
See map and information panel for Walk 18

•DISTANCE•	4½ miles (7.2km)
•MINIMUM TIME•	2hrs 15min
•ASCENT / GRADIENT•	131ft (40m)
•LEVEL OF DIFFICULTY•	

Walk 19 Directions (Walk 18 option)

Leave the car park by the path signposted to the village. At the road, turn left, walk past the church and turn right opposite the vicarage. Turn left at **Hunter's House**, walk down the drive. Tucked away behind the church, is **Avebury Manor**. Originally a monastery, the present building dates from the early 16th century. Some of the rooms are open to the public. Outside the Manor, don't miss the exquisite flower and topiary gardens.

Cross a footbridge and a further bridge before forking right. In 50yds (46m), climb the stile on your right, Point Ⓐ, and proceed ahead to cross a footbridge via stiles. Bear left across the field to a stile, head straight across the next field to double stiles then maintain direction across the following large field. Negotiate three stiles at the field boundary and follow the left-hand edge of a water-meadow to a stile, Point Ⓑ. Turn left through a gate and ascend along the right-hand field edge to a gate. Continue uphill to a gate on to **Windmill Hill** (Point Ⓒ).

Enclosing about 21 acres (8.5ha), Windmill Hill is one of Britain's largest neolithic causeway enclosures, consisting of three concentric ditches overlying an earlier settlement. It was a seasonal gathering place for the settlers in the Marlborough Downs area in about 3300 BC. Between the inner ditches you can see a bowl barrow and a bell barrow which form part of a small Bronze Age burial site of about 1700–1400 BC.

Walk through the earthworks, bear half-right beyond the two tumuli at the summit and keep to the right of a small wood. Go downhill to a gate. Turn left along the track, then fork right at the end of woodland into more open countryside. Follow the path to the left of a plantation and cross the stile on the left. Follow the left field edge, cross the double stiles on your left and continue along the right edge of the adjacent field. Cross a stile, maintain direction to a gate and along a fenced track. Bear sharp right, through a gate and turn left at a junction with a track, Point Ⓓ.

This track becomes **Bray Street**, narrows to a footpath and rejoins the outward journey by the footbridges. Retrace your steps back to the car park.

Walk 20

Barbury Castle

Explore a hill fort and enjoy the views on this downland ramble.

•DISTANCE•	4 miles (6.4km)
•MINIMUM TIME•	2hrs
•ASCENT / GRADIENT•	262ft (80m) ▲▲▲
•LEVEL OF DIFFICULTY•	林 林 林
•PATHS•	Tracks and byways, field paths, metalled lanes, 2 stiles
•LANDSCAPE•	Chalk downland
•SUGGESTED MAP•	aqua3 OS Explorer 169 Cirencester & Swindon
•START / FINISH•	Grid reference: SU 156760
•DOG FRIENDLINESS•	Let off lead in country park
•PARKING•	Free parking at Barbury Castle Country Park
•PUBLIC TOILETS•	Barbury Castle Country park

Walk 20 Directions

Some of the finest scenery in southern England can be found on the chalk downlands of Wiltshire, in particular the Marlborough Downs, which extend south from Swindon across the Vale of Pewsey to the northern flanks of Salisbury Plain. These expansive landscapes, with their wide skies and smooth ridges interspersed with long shallow combes, have captured the imagination of many writers, including Richard Jefferies whose lyrical prose was deeply influenced by the vast open downland and the far-reaching views. His favoured spot along the northern ridge of the Marlborough Downs was on Barbury Down where he could stroll the lofty tracks and savour the breathtaking views across the Vale

of the White Horse to the Cotswolds. About 150 acres (61ha) of open land on Barbury Down have been designated a country park by Wiltshire County Council.

The archaeology of the area is renowned, with a mass of ancient field monuments, including stone circles, post-Roman earthworks, field systems, burial mounds and hill forts, littering the landscape. During the Iron Age, a succession of tribes invaded Britain, many of them settling on the North Wessex Downs where they constructed dramatic hill forts on the downland escarpments, away from the threat of advancing enemies. One of the best known hill forts in southern England provides the focal point of the country park and our walk.

Barbury Castle is a well-defined oval of about 12 acres (5ha), with entrances at the eastern and western sides passing through towering double ramparts, as well as ditches and other defences, which may have been added when it was re-fortified in the Saxon period. Finds from the

---

WHERE TO EAT AND DRINK ⓘ
Light refreshments are available at the warden's hut and, on fine days in summer, there may be an ice cream van in the car park. Nearby pubs include the **Bell Inn** and the **Crown** in Broad Hinton.

Walk 20

WHILE YOU'RE THERE ⓘ

Take a closer look at one of Wiltshire's eight white horse chalk figures. South along the Ridgeway path, and accessible by car via Broad Hinton, is the **Hackpen White Horse**, a figure 29.5yds (27m) high cut in 1837 to celebrate Queen Victoria's coronation.

site suggest that it was used over a long period of time and include flint axes, Iron-Age and Roman pottery, weapons, tools and jewellery. You can see many of these on display in Devizes Museum. Half a mile (800m) north of the castle lies the battlefield of Beranburth where Saxon chief Cynric and his son Ceawlin defeated the Britons in a bloody massacre. It established the Saxons as overlords of southern England and later, in AD 560, Ceawlin became King of Wessex,

From the car park, turn right and continue past the viewing point to a gate. Continue along the **Ridgeway** to the eastern entrance and enter the **hill fort**. Walk around the rampart or walk straight across the centre to leave via the western entrance. Turn right down a lane and in 50yds (45m), turn right at the crossing of ways and walk along the gravel track signposted '**Ridgeway Route for Vehicles**'.

Used for over 4,000 years, the Ridgeway linked East Anglia with the Dorset coast. The official long distance trail begins at Ivinghoe Beacon in Buckinghamshire and follows the chalk ridges to Avebury 85 miles (137km) away.

At the T-Junction, turn right up the metalled lane and in 250yds (229m), turn left along the waymarked bridleway. Head across the field in the direction of the

aerial on the horizon. Eventually join a track opposite a building in a wooded enclosure. Follow the track past **Barbury Shooting School** then, at the end of the track, bear half-right towards the gap in a line of trees on the brow of the hill. At the crest bear left with the '**Millennium Trail Bridleway**' waymark. At the angled junction, turn sharp right, signposted '**Millennium Trail Byway**'.

Steeply ascend **Burderop Down** to a stile and gate and continue to climb along the left-hand edge of a large field, pausing to read the memorial stone to Alfred Williams and Richard Jeffries on your right. Writer and journalist Richard Jefferies (1848–87), who was born at Coate near Swindon, is perhaps Wiltshire's best-known country writer. He spent much of his time walking the Wiltshire Downs and wrote: 'They only know a country who are acquainted with its footpaths. By the roads, indeed, the outside may be seen; but the footpaths go through the heart of the land'. His plaque on the stone faces his birthplace. On the other side of the memorial stone a plaque is dedicated to Alfred Williams (1877–1930), self-taught scholar, linguist and nature poet who was born at nearby South Marston.

Eventually reach a stile and turn left up the lane. Shortly, turn right back into the car park, or keep straight on to visit the shop and café.

WHAT TO LOOK FOR ⓘ

As you traverse Burderop Down look for the outline of the 'Celtic' **field system** covering about 140 acres (56.7ha) of downland. Banks define the rectangular fields which were used from the Iron Age to medieval times.

The Infant Thames at Cricklade

An easy ramble across water-meadows beside the Thames and disused canals from Wiltshire's northernmost town.

•DISTANCE•	5½ miles (8.8km)
•MINIMUM TIME•	2hrs 30min
•ASCENT / GRADIENT•	Negligible
•LEVEL OF DIFFICULTY•	
•PATHS•	Field paths and bridle paths, disused railway, town streets, 15 stiles
•LANDSCAPE•	Flat river valley
•SUGGESTED MAP•	aqua3 OS Explorer 169 Cirencester & Swindon
•START / FINISH•	Grid reference: SU 100934
•DOG FRIENDLINESS•	Dogs can be off lead along old railway line
•PARKING•	Cricklade Town Hall car park (free)
•PUBLIC TOILETS•	Cricklade High Street

BACKGROUND TO THE WALK

The River Thames begins life in a peaceful Gloucestershire field near Cirencester. Before long it graduates to a sizeable stream, also known as the Isis at this point, on its way to the Cotswold Water Park, a vast network of lakes and pools, before reaching Cricklade, Wiltshire's northernmost town and the only one situated on the river.

Although merely a meandering willow-fringed stream as it passes through the town, research in the 19th-century revealed that the river at Cricklade had been navigable by barges weighing up to six tons during the 17th and 18th centuries. In 1607 the Burcot Commission was established for the purpose of improving the Thames as a navigable waterway from Clifton Hampden to Cricklade. Thomas Baskerville, writing in 1690, commented: 'So farewell Cricklade, come off ye ground, we'll sail in boats, towards London Town, for this is now the highest station by famous Tems for Navigation'. With the completion of the Thames and Severn Canal in 1789 river traffic was transferred to the canal and the upper reaches of the Thames gradually became overgrown.

Cricklade – Roman Military Post

Cricklade's advantageous position at the junction of four ancient roads may well be why it was established as the head of the navigable Thames. However, Cricklade's importance as a settlement began in Roman times when it was an important military post on Ermine Street, the Roman road linking Cirencester and Silchester. Evidence of the Roman's occupation has been found in and around the town, with villas to the north and south east. The later fortified Saxon town was built as a defence against the Danes and had its own mint. Today, the wide High Street has worthy buildings from the 17th and 18th centuries and two contrasting parish churches. You should not miss St Sampson's, characterised by its cathedral-like turreted tower which rises high above the town and dominates the surrounding water-meadows.

Abandoned Communication Lines

This walk follows the River Thames north, away from Cricklade, via the Thames Path. Beyond North Meadow, your route passes beside a shallow ditch that was once the North Wilts Canal, which opened in 1819 and ran the 9 miles (14.5km) between Swindon and Latton, linking the Wilts and Berks Canal with the Thames and Severn Canal. Soon you will follow the old tow path beside the muddy, weed-clogged ditch that was once the Thames and Severn Canal, opened in 1789 to link the River Severn with the Thames at Lechlade. The canal closed to all traffic in 1927, and was finally abandoned in 1933. Later the walk heads south along a disused railway line, part of the Midland and South West Railway which was closed to passengers in 1961. Although a pleasing reminder of the railway era, the ever-present drone of traffic from the A419 across the water-meadows keeps the mind firmly in the 21st century.

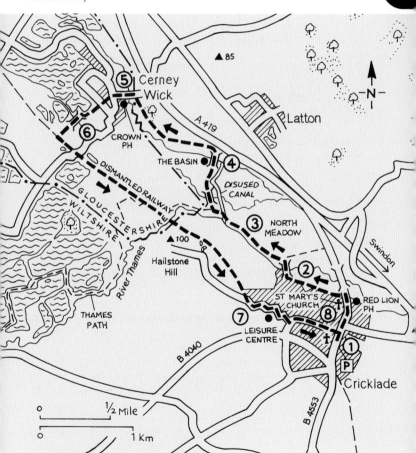

Walk 21 **Directions**

❶① Turn right out of the car park, keep ahead at the roundabout and walk along the **High Street**.

Pass **St Mary's Church**, then turn left along **North Wall** before the river bridge. Shortly, bear right to a stile and join the **Thames Path**. Cross a stile and continue along the field

Walk 21

WHERE TO EAT AND DRINK ℹ
You will find various pubs/hotels, notably the **Red Lion** near the Thames, and a traditional café in Cricklade. At the halfway point on the walk, at Cerney Wick, the family-owned **Crown** offers traditional home-cooked food, real ales and a large garden.

edge to houses.

② Go through the kissing gate on your right and bear left across the field to a gate. Follow the fenced footpath, cross a plank bridge and pass through the gate immediately on your right-hand side. Cross the river bridge and turn left through a gate. Walk beside the infant **River Thames**, crossing two stiles to enter **North Meadow**.

③ Continue to cross a stile by a bridge. Go through the gate immediately right and keep straight ahead, ignoring the Thames Path left. Follow the path beside the disused canal. Cross a footbridge and two stiles then, at a fence, bear right to cross a footbridge close to a house named **The Basin**. Cross a stile and bear right along the drive.

④ Cross a bridge and turn left through the gateway. Shortly, bear right to join the path along the left side of the old canal. Keep to the path for ½ mile (800m) to the road. Turn left into **Cerney Wick** to reach a T-junction.

⑤ Cross the stile opposite and keep ahead through the paddock to a

stone stile and lane. Cross the lane and climb the stile opposite, continuing ahead to a further stile. In a few paces, cross the stile on the right and follow the path beside a lake. Bear right, then left and bear off left (yellow arrow) into trees where the path becomes a track.

⑥ Cross a footbridge and proceed ahead along the field edge to a stile. Turn left along the old railway, signed 'Cricklade'. Cross the **River Thames** in a mile (1.6km) and keep to the path along the former

WHILE YOU'RE THERE ℹ
Visit Cricklade's small local **museum** where collections, photographs and maps illustrate the history of the town from the Roman era to the present day. Head for the attractive village of Ashton Keynes and the heart of the **Cotswold Water Park**, Britain's largest water park, with 133 lakes providing water sports, nature trails and a visitor centre at **Keynes Country Park**.

trackbed to a bridge.

⑦ Follow the gravel path to the **Leisure Centre**. Bear left on to the road, following it right, then turn left opposite the entrance to the Leisure Centre car park. Turn right, then next left and follow the road to the church.

⑧ Walk beside the barrier and turn left in front of **The Gatehouse** into the churchyard. Bear left to the main gates and follow the lane to a T-junction. Turn right to make your

WHAT TO LOOK FOR ℹ
Walk across **North Meadow**, a National Nature Reserve, in spring to see many rare plants and flowers, including Britain's largest area of rare snakeshead fritillaries. At **Cerney Wick**, note the restored lock and the well-preserved roundhouse, originally the home of the lengthsman whose job was to look after the canal, ensuring that the level of water did not drop below the necessary minimum. In Cricklade, look for the Victorian **Jubilee Clock** in the High Street and the medieval carved crosses in both churchyards.

Dinton and the Nadder Valley

Enjoy the varied scenery, the architecture and the history of two delightful villages as you explore the unspoilt Nadder Valley.

•DISTANCE•	5¼ miles (8.4km)
•MINIMUM TIME•	3hrs
•ASCENT / GRADIENT•	360ft (110m) ▲▲▲
•LEVEL OF DIFFICULTY•	👥 👥 👥
•PATHS•	Tracks, field and woodland paths, parkland, 15 stiles
•LANDSCAPE•	River valley and wooded hillside
•SUGGESTED MAP•	aqua3 OS Explorer 130 Salisbury & Stonehenge
•START / FINISH•	Grid reference: SU 009315
•DOG FRIENDLINESS•	Dogs can be off lead in Dinton Park
•PARKING•	Dinton Park National Trust car park
•PUBLIC TOILETS•	None on route

BACKGROUND TO THE WALK

The Nadder Valley is quite unlike any of the other river valleys that radiate out from Salisbury, for it is not a distinct deep valley incised in the chalk strata as is evident in the neighbouring Ebble and Wylye river valleys. This anomalous character is due to the fact that the Nadder traverses a sequence of rock types, resulting in a landscape of scarp slopes and deep combes within its broad vale. In this well-watered valley, villages free from the need to be located on the banks of the Nadder, are found scattered across the landscape, nestling among lush meadows, wooded hills and along gentle tributary streams. Your walk explores the heart of the Nadder Valley, its wooded slopes and two unspoilt villages, delightful Dinton and the charmingly named Compton Chamberlayne.

Dinton's Famous Families

The village of Dinton, built on a hillside north of the Nadder, is bordered by three beautifully landscaped houses, each associated with important Wiltshire families. Surprisingly for such a small village, the National Trust owns four properties here – Hyde's House, Lawes Cottage, Little Clarendon and Philipps House – the latter two are open to the public during the summer months. In the old part of the village, close to St Mary's Church, you will find Hyde's House, an elegant building with a Queen Anne façade masking 16th-century origins. It was here that Charles II's chancellor, Edward Hyde was born in 1609.

His daughter Anne married the future James II and was mother to Queen Anne and Queen Mary. Close to the village shop is Lawes Cottage, the 17th-century home of the Lawes family. Henry Lawes (1596–1662) was a well known musician and composer of the day. He became Master of the King's Musick, wrote the anthem for the Coronation of Charles II and, as a friend of Milton, wrote the music for his *Masque of Comus* in 1634. Next door is Little Clarendon, a handsome, early Tudor manor house with a small 20th-century chapel in the garden. You can view three ground floor rooms, each furnished with vernacular oak furniture. The grandest of all the houses is Philipps House, an imposing stone mansion with a neo-Grecian façade that dominates Dinton Park. Formerly called Dinton House, it was completed in 1820 by Jeffrey Wyatt for William Wyndham, the last of the three great families to reside in Dinton.

The Penruddockes of Compton Chamberlayne

Overlooking a lovely lake in peaceful parkland, Compton House (not open to the public) was the seat of the Penruddockes, an influential Wiltshire family for 300 years from 1550. The small 13th-century church contains the family vault and the remains of John Penruddocke, a gallant gentleman who was executed in 1655 following his efforts to raise support against Parliamentarian rule.

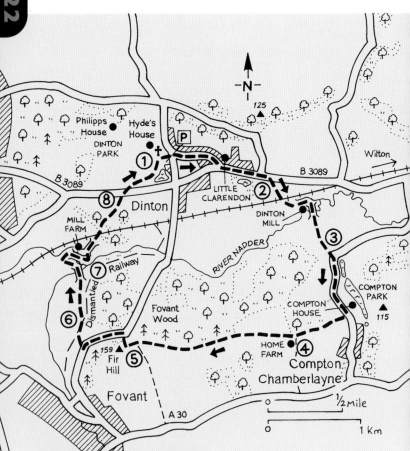

Walk 22 **Directions**

① Leave the car park, cross and follow the lane to the **B3089**. Turn left, pass **Little Clarendon**, and continue for ¼ mile (400m). Take the path right by a bus shelter.

② Follow the track to a kissing gate and cross the railway line to a further gate. Keep to the track and bear left alongside a stream to reach **Dinton Mill**. Pass to the left of the mill, cross the footbridge over the **River Nadder** and follow the drive to a lane.

Walk 22

③ Turn right and follow the metalled lane into **Compton Chamberlayne**. Take the footpath right, opposite the entrance to **Compton House**. Steadily ascend, pass round a gate and continue along the track to **Home Farm** and a junction of tracks.

④ Turn right, follow the track left around farm buildings and remain on the track with views of the regimental badges. Walk beside woodland, then on nearing the field corner, follow the narrow path into the trees and continue close to the woodland fringe. Pass a reservoir to reach a track.

⑤ Turn right and walk downhill to a lane. Turn left then, at the sharp left bend, take the path right and enter a field (stile left). Bear half right to a stile. Cross a track, pass

through a kissing gate and walk across rough grassland, soon to bear left to a gate.

⑥ Turn right along the field edge, go through a kissing gate and bear left down the right-hand side of a field. At a waymarker, follow the path left, downhill to a stile. Descend through scrub, cross a footbridge, then a stile and walk ahead to a further stile. Bear left along the riverbank, cross a stile and continue to a bridge over the mill stream.

⑦ Pass in front of **Mill Farm** on a permissive path. Cross a footbridge and stile and bear diagonally right towards the railway. Cross the line via stiles and bear slightly right to a stile and woodland. Walk through to a stile and keep ahead, to the rear of a barn, to a stile. Continue ahead to a stile, then cut across pasture, keeping to the right of the second telegraph pole to a stile and road.

⑧ Cross the stile opposite into **Dinton Park** and turn right alongside the hedge. Bear off left along a grassy path, pass the pond and head towards the church. Go through the first gate on your right and return to the car park.

Old and New Wardour Castles

A gentle ramble through the serene Nadder Valley and rolling parkland around romantic medieval ruins.

•DISTANCE•	3½ miles (5.7km)
•MINIMUM TIME•	1hr 30min
•ASCENT / GRADIENT•	278ft (85m) ▲ ▲ ▲
•LEVEL OF DIFFICULTY•	🚶 🚶 🚶
•PATHS•	Field and woodland paths, parkland tracks, 13 stiles
•LANDSCAPE•	River valley, undulating parkland
•SUGGESTED MAP•	aqua3 OS Explorer 118 Shaftesbury & Cranborne Chase
•START / FINISH•	Grid reference: ST 938264
•DOG FRIENDLINESS•	Dogs can be off lead on downland track (Walk 24)
•PARKING•	Free parking at Old Wardour Castle
•PUBLIC TOILETS•	Old Wardour Castle (if visiting ruin)

BACKGROUND TO THE WALK

The austere ruins of Old Wardour Castle stand in a truly romantic and peaceful lakeside setting deep in south Wiltshire countryside. On a spur of high ground, protected by acres of secluded woodland, they overlook the Palladian mansion of New Wardour Castle and the tranquil Nadder Valley.

Unique Design

Old Wardour was constructed in 1393 for John, 5th Lord Lovel of Titchmarsh and remodelled in 1578 by Sir Matthew Arundell. It was not built as a fortress in the familiar sense of the word but as a tower house as much for comfort and lavish entertainment as for defence. There is no other castle like it in England, hexagonal in shape and with all its rooms and chambers contained within the one building. This unique design is thought to have been inspired by similar structures in France, where Lord Lovel had been campaigning during the Hundred Years War.

Civil War Sieges

During the Civil War in 1643 the castle had to be defended against a Commonwealth army. A garrison of only 50 soldiers and servants, along with Lady Arundell, conducted an heroic defence of Old Wardour, holding out for six days against 1,300 of Cromwell's regulars led by Sir Edward Hungerford. The Parliamentarian leader was notorious for depriving the most prominent Royalist families of their houses and property. Lady Arundell surrendered only when offered honourable terms, which the Roundheads immediately broke, sacking the castle and imprisoning her.

Rather than destroy the castle, the Parliamentarians decided to install a garrison there and use it to protect themselves from a strengthening Royalist army in Wiltshire. However, Henry, Lord Arundell's son, resolved to recover his confiscated property and his home. After several unsuccessful demands for the Parliamentarians to surrender, the young Arundell lay siege to the castle in January 1644. During the siege a gunpowder mine was laid in a drainage tunnel underneath the castle. When it exploded a large portion of the structure collapsed, leaving it uninhabitable.

Romantic Ruin

Old Wardour was never restored after the war, the Arundell's content to build a smaller house on the south side of the bailey wall. In the early 18th century the ruins were surrounded by landscaped gardens, creating the flavour of a romantic ruin. Film buffs may recognise the castle as it was used extensively during the filming of *Robin Hood: Prince of Thieves* (1991). New Wardour Castle was designed in a Palladian style by James Paine for the 8th Lord Arundell and built, between 1769 and 1776, on the other side of the park. It remained the seat of the Arundell family until 1944. This fine building has since been a school and has recently been converted into apartments.

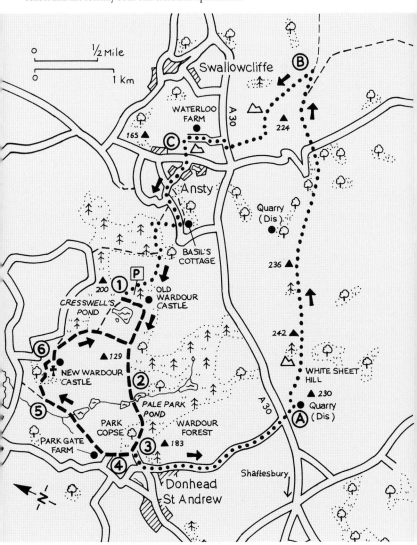

Walk 23 Directions

① From the parking area turn left along the drive and pass between the castle and **Cresswell's Pond**. Pass the **Gothic Pavilion**, then at **Wardour House** (private) bear right with the trackway. Gently climb the wide track, skirting woodland, then at a fork keep right. At the end of the woodland, cross a stile by a field entrance and walk ahead along the right-hand side of the field, heading downhill to a stile.

WHILE YOU'RE THERE ℹ️

Visit nearby **Tisbury** and its magnificent 15th-century stone tithe barn, which at nearly 200ft (61m) long is reputedly the largest in England.

---

② Follow the path beside **Pale Park Pond** to a further stile, then ascend across the field to a stile and woodland. Shortly, bear left, then right to join the main forest track. Keep right at a fork and soon leave **Wardour Forest**, passing beside a gate on to a gravel drive.

③ At the end of the drive cross the stile on your right. (For Walk 24 keep ahead along the track). Head downhill across the field to a metal gate and follow the waymarked path through **Park Copse**, soon to bear left down a grassy clearing to

---

WHAT TO LOOK FOR ℹ️

Explore the grounds of **Old Wardour Castle** and locate the elaborate rockwork grotto and the miniature replica of the Avebury stone circle, both part of the 18th-century landscaping improvements. On Walk 24, look out for the well-preserved **milestone** at the top of White Sheet Hill, dated 1736, providing evidence that the track was once the old highway to London.

---

a stile beside a field entrance. Follow the right-hand edge towards **Park Gate Farm**.

④ Cross a stile on to the farm drive and turn right (yellow arrow) to cross the concrete farmyard to a gate. Follow the path beside the hedge to a further gate, with the **River Nadder** on the left, then proceed ahead along the right-hand field edge to a stile. Bear diagonally left across the field, aiming for the left-hand side of a cottage. Go through a gate and maintain direction to reach a stile.

⑤ Cross the farm drive and the stile opposite and head straight uphill, keeping left of the tree, towards a stile and woodland. Follow the path right through the trees and soon bear left to pass a building on your left. **New Wardour Castle** is visible on your right. Keep close to the bushes across the grounds towards the main drive and turn right along a gravel path and follow the sign 'Chapel'.

⑥ Join the drive and walk past **New Wardour Castle**. Where the track forks, keep right to a stile beside a gate. Follow the grassy track ahead across parkland towards **Old Wardour Castle**. Climb a stile beside a gate and proceed ahead, following the track uphill to a T-junction of tracks. Turn left and follow your outward route back to the car park.

WHERE TO EAT AND DRINK ℹ️

Tea and coffee are available if visiting **Old Wardour Castle**. There are no refreshments on either of the walk options, but White Sheet Hill makes a good picnic spot with a view. A short detour in Donhead St Andrew will lead you to the **Foresters Inn**.

White Sheet Hill and Ansty

A longer walk along a breezy downland track to secluded Ansty.
See map and information panel for Walk 23

•DISTANCE•	8 miles (12.9km)
•MINIMUM TIME•	4hrs
•ASCENT / GRADIENT•	787ft (240m) ▲▲▲
•LEVEL OF DIFFICULTY•	🚶🚶🚶

Walk 24 Directions (Walk 23 option)

Having walked to the end of the drive, Point ③, continue along the track to a lane and turn left through **Donhead St Andrew** for 1 mile (1.6km) to the **A30**, Point Ⓐ. Cross over and ascend the zig-zag track up **White Sheet Hill**. Continue for 1¼ miles (2km) to a road.

The ancient highway up White Sheet Hill follows the crest of chalk downland all the way to Salisbury. Centuries ago it provided dry passage for pilgrims travelling from Salisbury to the abbeys at Wilton and Shaftesbury. In later years it formed part of the coach road from the West Country to London, before the turnpike at the base of the hill.

Cross the road and follow the track for ½ mile (800m) to a waymarker, Point Ⓑ. Bear left across the field to gate and turn left to a further gate. Where the fence veers left, bear off right steeply downhill to join a path that descends the scarp face at an angle. Go through two gates in the field corner and turn left through a further gate. Turn right along the field edge to a stile and continue to a gate and the **A30**. Turn right, then left along the drive towards **Waterloo Farm**. Pass between barns, join a track and take the footpath left just before a gate. Pass a gate on your right, then take the path right and steeply descend into **Ansty**, Point Ⓒ.

Ansty has long been associated with royalty since Alfred and successive kings of Wessex hunted in the surrounding forests. In 1211 the manor title deeds were given to the Knights Hospitallers of the Order of St John of Jerusalem. A Preceptory was formed and they built the Church of St James, the fishpond and a hospice for pilgrims on their way to Shaftesbury Abbey. You can still see the pond, the church and Ansty Manor.

At the lane turn left to see the **Preceptory**. Otherwise, take the lane opposite and follow it for ½ mile (800m), passing **Basil's Cottage**, then take the path right, across a stile beside a house. Walk uphill towards woodland. Bear right to a stile on the woodland edge. Proceed ahead and turn left on meeting a track. Keep left at a junction and follow the track right to a crossing of paths. Continue ahead along a fenced path between fields. Enter woodland and descend the track ahead to the car park.

Ebble Valley Wanderings

Enjoy the unspoilt rural landscape of the upper Ebble Valley.

•DISTANCE•	5 miles (8km)
•MINIMUM TIME•	2hrs 30min
•ASCENT / GRADIENT•	377ft (115m) ▲▲▲
•LEVEL OF DIFFICULTY•	林林 林林 林林
•PATHS•	Byways, field paths, bridle paths, metalled lanes, 8 stiles
•LANDSCAPE•	Chalk downland and river valley
•SUGGESTED MAP•	aqua3 OS Explorer 118 Shaftesbury & Cranborne Chase
•START / FINISH•	Grid reference: ST 964250
•DOG FRIENDLINESS•	Let dogs off lead along downland track
•PARKING•	On top of Swallowcliffe Down
•PUBLIC TOILETS•	None on route

Walk 25 Directions

Of all the valleys that radiate out from Salisbury, the Ebble must be the most peaceful and unspoilt. Time seems to have passed by the valley and its string of tranquil villages, for it's free from busy main roads and their associated developments. This is particularly true in the upper Ebble Valley close to Cranborne Chase and the Dorset border where the 13 mile (21km) long chalk stream rises. Here, tortuous narrow lanes link isolated farmsteads, hamlets and villages, hidden and protected in the folds of the steeply rising chalk hills.

Head west along the arrowed byway. Emerge from the copse and take the bridleway left. Descend into the **Ebble Valley**, keeping to the narrow path beside the fence to a gate. Continue ahead down the field edge, following the track through two gates to **Norrington Manor**. Cross the track and walk between farm buildings. Norrington Manor and the nearby village of

Alvediston date back to medieval times when they were associated with one of the oldest families in England, the Gawens, said to be descended from the legendary knight Sir Gawain of King Arthur's Round Table. The original manor house was built in the time of Richard II and the Gawens completed the building after 1377. Much of the striking 14th-century stone building still stands with some 17th-century additions.

Where the track veers right, cross the stile on your left and keep to the left-hand field edge to a stile in the corner. Cross the track and take the path ahead through the valley bottom to a gate. Keep left-handed through the field to a stile and lane in **Alvediston**. Turn right, then left along the drive to **St Mary's Church**. Continue along the lane to visit the **Crown Inn**.

Memorials to the Gawen family, and the Wyndham family who succeeded them at Norrington after 450 years, can be seen in the church which was rebuilt in 1866 and overlooks peaceful water-meadows. Pride of place at the front of the churchyard is the tomb of Sir Anthony Eden (1897–1977), Earl of Avon and Prime Minister between 1955 and 1957. He lived in the brick-built 18th-century manor house close to the church.

Go through the gate on your right and keep to the path ahead across two fields to a gate and enter **West End**. At the road, turn right across the bridge, then immediately left and follow the lane to a fork. Bear left along **Duck Street**, then as it begins to dip left, fork right along a footpath to the church in **Ebbesbourne Wake**.

Ebbesbourne Wake nestles beside the intermittently flowing Ebble stream at the base of the downs, oblivious to 21st-century hustle and bustle. A collection of neat thatched cottages congregate around the 15th-century church, which stands on a hill, and close to the gem of a simple and unspoilt village inn – the Horseshoe.

By the lychgate, bear left to the lane and turn right to visit the **Horseshoe**. Otherwise, turn left down **Duck Street**, take the path right, cross the bridge over the **Ebble** and climb the stile on your left. Follow the path diagonally right up to a stile. Cross the stile opposite and bear left along the field edge. Climb steadily, go through the gate on the left and

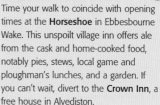

> **WHERE TO EAT AND DRINK**
> Time your walk to coincide with opening times at the **Horseshoe** in Ebbesbourne Wake. This unspoilt village inn offers ale from the cask and home-cooked food, notably pies, stews, local game and ploughman's lunches, and a garden. If you can't wait, divert to the **Crown Inn**, a free house in Alvediston.

continue ascending along a track to a gate. Follow the field edge, cross two stiles, then bear right along a bridleway. At a crossing of tracks, turn left and follow it back to the car parking area.

For hundreds, even thousands of years, this hilltop track, known as the Herepath or the Salisbury Way, was one of main highways linking Salisbury to the west, especially for pilgrims travelling to the abbeys at Wilton and Shaftesbury. In later years the route was used by horse-drawn coaches en route from London to Exeter, until improved road-making techniques in the 19th century made it possible for a new road to be built in the Nadder Valley. Its importance in the earliest of days can be traced through the presence of earthworks, barrows, tumuli and a little way east, the Iron-Age settlement of Chiselbury Camp. It is now a deserted grassy track providing a fine panorama to the north across the broad, undulating and wooded Nadder Valley, and south down steep dry valleys into the narrow Ebble Valley to lofty chalk downland beyond.

> **WHILE YOU'RE THERE**
> Take a leisurely drive through the delightful **Ebble Valley**. Begin at Berwick St James and head east through Ebbesbourne Wake to Fifield Bavant and visit **St Martin's Church**, one of England's smallest churches measuring 35ft (10.6m) long and 15ft (4.5m) wide. In Broad Chalke, the largest village in the valley, you will see some fine manor houses, notably **Reddish House** where the photographer and designer Sir Cecil Beaton lived until his death in 1980. He is buried in the churchyard.

Exploring Bowood Park

Combine a visit to one of Wiltshire's grandest houses with a walk across its landscaped parkland and along a disued railway.

•DISTANCE•	7 miles (11.3km)
•MINIMUM TIME•	3hrs 30min
•ASCENT / GRADIENT•	360ft (110m) ▲▲▲
•LEVEL OF DIFFICULTY•	👫 👫 👫
•PATHS•	Field, woodland and parkland paths, metalled drives, pavement beside A4, former railway line, 3 stiles
•LANDSCAPE•	Rolling farmland and open parkland
•SUGGESTED MAP•	aqua3 OS Explorer 156 Chippenham & Bradford-on-Avon
•START / FINISH•	Grid reference: ST 998710
•DOG FRIENDLINESS•	Keep dogs under contol; off lead along former railway
•PARKING•	Choice of car parks in Calne
•PUBLIC TOILETS•	Calne

BACKGROUND TO THE WALK

Like many north Wiltshire towns, Calne rose to fame producing woollen broadcloth and, up until the 18th century, the town had 20 or more mills along the River Marden. Even St Mary's Church owes its splendour to the generous donations of the rich clothiers and wool merchants in the 15th century. When the Industrial Revolution killed its livelihood, Calne turned to bacon-curing and the making of sausages and pies, although meat processing had been a major employer in the town from the early 19th century, thanks to its location. Calne was a resting place on the main droving route from the West Country to Smithfield Market. Cattle, sheep and, more importantly pigs, which had been transported from Ireland via Bristol, passed through the town. Harris, the family butchers, took their pick from the grunting mass, eventually establishing their factory here, and in 1864 patented their bacon-curing process. Calne became the home of Wiltshire bacon and further prospered with the arrival of the railway. Now both the railway and Harris have gone leaving this busy crossroads town with a faded air, although an ambitious plan for reconstructing the town centre is now taking shape. Around the Green are the finest of Calne's Georgian houses, especially Adam House and Bentley House, classic reminders that Calne was once a prosperous market town.

Bowood House

With little to encourage you to linger, leave the town and the busy A4 and head west to the tranquil parkland that surrounds Bowood House, the true focus of your walk. Scenic footpaths take you through the 1,000 acres (405ha) of beautiful parkland, skirting the lake, pleasure gardens and the handsome Georgian house. Originally built in 1624, the house was unfinished when it was bought by the first Earl of Shelburne in 1764. He employed some of the greatest British architects of the day, notably Robert Adam, to design the Diocletion Wing containing the library, galleries, conservatories, a laboratory and a chapel, while 'Capability' Brown laid out the gardens, which are regarded as his best surviving and most satisfactory creations.

Walk 26

In 1955 the original portion of this once magnificent palace had to be demolished, the Lansdownes sacrificing 200 rooms to create a habitable home and preserve the rest of their inheritance. What is left is still impressive, housing a remarkable collection of family heirlooms and works of art. The chief glory of Bowood, however, lies in its pleasure gardens, carpeted with daffodils, narcissi and bluebells in spring. Lawns roll gently down to a long tranquil lake, and there are cascades, caves and grottoes, while terraces, roses, clipped hedges and sculptures are a perfect complement to the house. If you are walking this way between mid-May and mid-June, make sure you explore the spectacular rhododendron walks, over 2 miles (3.2km) long and not to be missed.

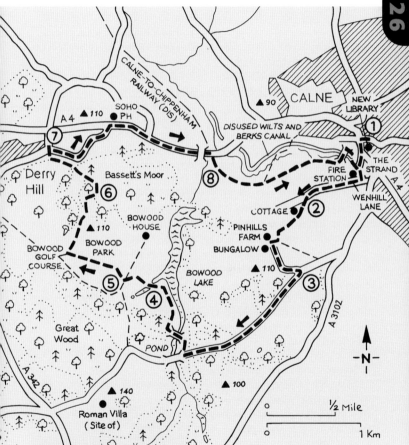

Walk 26 Directions

① Locate the new library on **The Strand** (A4) and walk south along **New Road** to the roundabout. Turn right along **Station Road** and take the metalled footpath left opposite the fire station. Turn right on

reaching **Wenhill Lane** and follow it out of the built-up area.

② On nearing a cottage, follow the waymarker left and walk along the field edge. Just beyond the cottage, climb the bank and keep left along the field edge to a plank bridge and stile. Keep to the left-hand field

Walk 26

WHAT TO LOOK FOR ⓘ
As you stroll around The Green in Calne, look for the wall plaque on **Bentley House**, near the church, stating that Samuel Taylor Coleridge lived and wrote here between 1814 and 1816. Note the old **water pump** beside the A4 in Calne which was used to lay the dust when New Road was built in 1801. **Black Dog Halt** is one of many names in Wiltshire associated with Black Dog folklore.

WHERE TO EAT AND DRINK ⓘ
There are various pubs and tea rooms in Calne, most notably the White Hart, and the **Soho** pub on the A4 which is open all day for food and drink. **Bowood House** has a licensed restaurant and self-service coffee shop. Just outside Calne, try the **White Horse** in Compton Bassett or the **Ivy** at Heddington.

edge and soon bear left to a stile. Follow the path right, through rough grass around **Pinhills Farm** to a stile opposite a bungalow and turn left along the drive.

③ At a junction, turn right along a further metalled drive and continue for a mile (1.6km). Near a bridge, take the footpath right, through a kissing gate and walk through parkland beside a pond. Cross a bridge, go through a gate and turn right alongside **Bowood Lake**.

④ Follow the path left to reach a gate and cross the causeway between lakes to a gate. Keep straight on up the track, following it left, then right to cross the driveway to **Bowood House**.

⑤ Beyond a gate, keep ahead along the field edge, soon to follow the path left straight across **Bowood Park**. Keep left of trees and the field boundary to a gate. Turn right along the metalled drive beside **Bowood Golf Course**. Where the drive turns sharp right to a cottage, keep straight on into woodland.

⑥ Follow the path left, downhill through a clearing (can be boggy) along the line of telegraph poles. Bear right with the path back into the woodland and soon follow it uphill beside the golf course. Turn

right through a break in the trees and go through the main gates to Bowood House into **Derry Hill**.

⑦ Turn immediately right along **Old Lane**. At the **A4**, turn right along the pavement. Shortly, cross to the opposite pavement and continue downhill. Pass beneath a footbridge and take the metalled drive immediately right.

⑧ Join the former Calne-to-Chippenham railway line at **Black Dog Halt**. Turn left and follow this back towards Calne. Cross the disused **Wilts and Berks Canal** and turn right along the tow path. Where the path forks keep right to reach **Station Road**. Retrace your steps to the town centre.

WHILE YOU'RE THERE ⓘ
Off the A4 just south of Calne you will find the **Atwell-Wilson Motor Museum**. It contains 100 vintage and classic cars from 1924 to 1983, including Cadillacs and a model 'T' Ford, motorbikes and unusual memorabilia.

Bremhill and Maud Heath's Causeway

Follow field paths to a hilltop monument and the start of Maud Heath's impressive Causeway.

•DISTANCE•	4 miles (6.4km)
•MINIMUM TIME•	1hr 30min
•ASCENT / GRADIENT•	295ft (90m) ▲▲▲
•LEVEL OF DIFFICULTY•	🚶🚶 🚶🚶 🚶🚶
•PATHS•	Field paths, bridle paths, metalled roads, 13 stiles
•LANDSCAPE•	Gently rolling farmland, downland escarpment
•SUGGESTED MAP•	aqua3 OS Explorer 156 Chippenham & Bradford-on-Avon
•START / FINISH•	Grid reference: ST 980730
•DOG FRIENDLINESS•	Keep dogs on leads at all times
•PARKING•	Bremhill church
•PUBLIC TOILETS•	None on route

BACKGROUND TO THE WALK

Nestling on the upper slopes of Wick Hill, surrounded by lush pastureland, isolated farmsteads and leafy lanes, tiny Bremhill is a timeless downland village complete with an ancient church, a fine stepped medieval cross and a single street lined with pretty ragstone cottages. Surprisingly, for such a pastoral area, there is much to interest the casual rambler undertaking this short walk, in addition to the absorbing views across the north Wiltshire plain to the Cotswold hills from the mile (1.6km) long stretch of bridle path across Wick Hill.

William Lisle Bowles – Rector and Poet

The Reverend William Lisle Bowles (1762–1850), rector of St Martin's Church in Bremhill from 1803 to 1844, lived in the vicarage, now Bremhill Court, adjacent to the church. Bowles was not only an eccentric, filling his garden with grottoes, urns and hermitages and keeping sheep in the churchyard with their bells tuned in thirds and fifths, he was also a poet. His literary friends, such as Wordsworth, Coleridge, Southey and Charles Lamb, were all part of the considerable literary circle centred upon Bowood House. Although much of his poetry was derided, it was his now forgotten sonnets, published in nine editions, that influenced the whole school of poetry and gained admiration from Coleridge and Wordsworth. Scour the churchyard and you will find some examples of Bowles' poetry, as this eccentric vicar was unable to resist breaking into verse on tombstones, monuments and even a sundial!

Maud Heath

One of Bowles' less impressive verses is inscribed on the monument you will pass on top of Wick Hill. Erected by Bowles and the Marquis of Lansdowne in 1838 it commemorates Maud Heath, a local widow, who in 1474 made a bequest of land and property in Chippenham to provide an income to build and maintain a causeway from Wick Hill through the Avon marshes to Chippenham, a distance of around 4½ miles (7.2km).

Although starting from the top of a hill, much of the land along the route was low lying and prone to flooding in winter, so her aim was to provide a dry pathway for country people to walk to market.

For much of its route the Causeway is little more than a raised path, but the most interesting section can be found at Kellaways, where the way is elevated some 6ft (1.8m) on stone arches as it crosses the River Avon, a remarkable feat of engineering for its time.

On top of the monument on Wick Hill, Maud is depicted in a shawl and bonnet with her basket by her side. Although she has been described as a market woman, it seems unlikely that a lady wealthy enough to provide land and property on this scale would have been walking to market herself. You will see the beginning of the Causeway as you cross the hilltop road, where a tablet states 'From this Wick Hill begins the praise of Maud Heath's gift to these highways'.

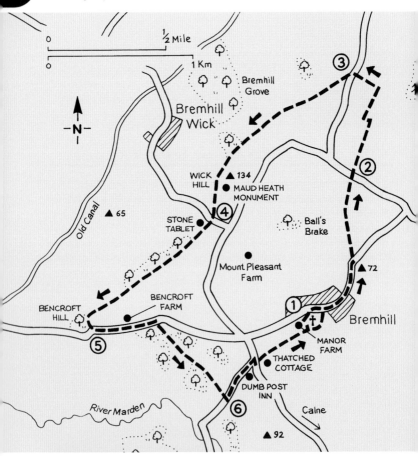

Walk 27 **Directions**

① With your back to the church, turn right and walk downhill through the village. Begin to climb and take the arrowed path left across the stile. Proceed straight on below the bank along the field edge to a stile in the corner. Bear diagonally right, uphill across the field to a gate and lane.

② Cross the stile opposite and cross a paddock to a further stile. Bear half-left to a stile in the field corner and walk along the left-hand edge to a gate and maintain direction to a stile. In the next field look out for and pass through a gate on your left and head straight across the field to a gate and lane.

③ Turn left, then immediately bear off right along a track to a gate. Join the waymarked bridle path along the right-hand field edge to a gate. Maintain direction through several fields and gates to reach the monument to Maud Heath on top of **Wick Hill**.

④ Continue to cross a lane via stiles, passing the stone tablet and inscription identifying the beginning of **Maud Heath's Causeway**. Follow the bridle path along the crest of the hill through seven fields via gates and bear left before woodland to reach a gate and lane at the top of **Bencroft Hill**.

⑤ Turn left, pass **Bencroft Farm** and a bungalow, then take the waymarked path right, through woodland to a gate. Continue ahead through a plantation, bearing left on nearing a gate to cross a stile.

Proceed straight across the field on a defined path, cross double fence stiles and remain on the path to a stile to the left of a bungalow.

⑥ Turn left along the lane, heading uphill to a junction beside the **Dumb Post Inn**. Turn right, then left along the drive to a thatched cottage. Go through a squeeze-stile and keep to the left-hand edge of the field through a gate and squeeze-stile to reach a stile in the field corner. Walk in front of **Manor Farm** to reach a gate leading into Bremhill churchyard. Bear right along the path back to your car.

Heytesbury Chalk Stream

A gentle stroll alongside the River Wylye and across lush water-meadows.

·DISTANCE·	4 miles (6.4km)
·MINIMUM TIME·	2hrs
·ASCENT / GRADIENT·	49ft (15m) ▲ ▲ ▲
·LEVEL OF DIFFICULTY·	🚶 🚶 🚶
·PATHS·	Field paths and bridleways, 10 stiles
·LANDSCAPE·	River valley and lofty chalk downland
·SUGGESTED MAP·	aqua3 OS Explorer 143 Warminster & Trowbridge
·START / FINISH·	Grid reference: ST 926425
·DOG FRIENDLINESS·	Keep dogs on lead on Walk 28; off lead on downland track of Walk 29
·PARKING·	Plenty of room along wide village street
·PUBLIC TOILETS·	None on route

BACKGROUND TO THE WALK

The River Wylye, one of Wiltshire's lesser-known chalk streams, threads its way through some of the finest downland scenery in the county on its 22 mile (35km) journey from Warminster to Salisbury. Iron-Age hill forts and ancient tumuli and barrows litter the rolling chalk downland, much of it now extensively farmed. In the valley, peacefully situated away from the A36, slumber pretty picture-postcard villages, including the charmingly named Knook, Boyton, Sherrington and Corton, all of which you will visit if you undertake the longer option, Walk 29.

Historic Heytesbury

Lying just 3 miles (4.8km) east of Warminster, the large village of Heytesbury is an ancient borough with a wealth of history and well worth allowing a little time for exploration before or after your walk, if you can resist the homely confines of the Angel Inn!

Wealth and prosperity came to the village through the prominence of one influential family in the 14th century – the Hungerfords – who acquired land and purchased manors across the south west, including a complex of manors in the upper Wylye Valley. Sir Walter Hungerford fought at Agincourt in 1415 and became Treasurer of England in 1428. He also founded and endowed a chapel in Salisbury Cathedral and founded the Almshouses, or Hospital of St John, that stand opposite the Angel Inn in the village. Under the Hungerfords, the Wylye estates became noted for sheep farming and Heytesbury became the main wool warehouse of the family, who were granted the right to hold a market and two yearly fairs.

Cloth production began in Heytesbury in the mid-15th century but it was not until the the 18th century that the proximity of the River Wylye attracted cloth mills along its course. Plans to develop the industry to match that of nearby Warminster never materialised and when its borough status was lost in the Great Reform Act of 1832 Heytesbury gradually declined, the population falling from 1,412 to a mere 454 by 1932.

Sadly, the village lacks buildings of any special interest due to the 'Great Fire' of 1765 which destroyed 65 dwellings along the main street. Notable exceptions include Heytesbury Mill, Parsonage Farm to the south of the church, 69 High Street and Heytesbury House, which stands across the A36 bypass on the site of the medieval mansion of East Court, once the home of the Hungerford family. In 1926 Heytesbury House became the home of the respected First World War poet and writer Siegfried Sassoon. He grew to love the dramatic views and wide horizons of Wiltshire's downland when he was stationed in the area during training on Salisbury Plain. This inspired him to buy Heytesbury Manor and following his death in 1967, it was occupied by his son George Sassoon until 1994.

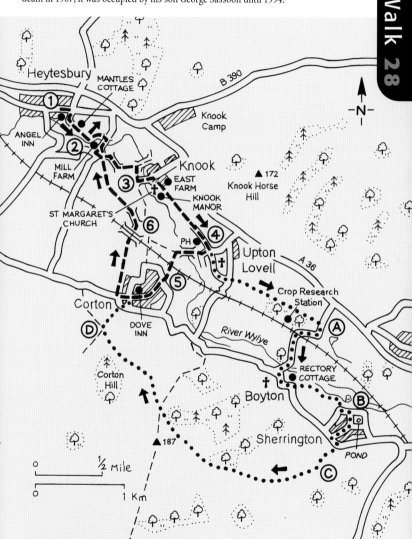

Walk 28 Directions

① Head east along the village street, pass the **Angel Inn** and turn right down **Mantles Lane**. Where it

curves right to become **Mill Lane**, take the footpath left along a drive beside the **River Wylye**. Bear right on to the footpath in front of **Mantles Cottage**, go through a walk-through stile and walk along the right-hand edge of pasture, soon to bear slightly left on nearing **Mill Farm** to reach a gate.

② Beyond a further gate, turn right across the bridge, then follow the yellow arrow left and soon cross a footbridge. Follow the **Wessex Ridgeway** marker straight ahead at a junction of ways then, just before a further footbridge, turn left through a gap and bear right along the field edge. At a white wooden arrow, bear half left across the field towards thatched cottages to the riverbank and bear right to a stile and junction of paths.

③ Turn left across the footbridge, pass **Knook Manor** and **St Margaret's Church**, then turn right by the post-box and soon pass **East Farm** on a track (which can be very messy after rain). At two gates, go through the left-hand gate and proceed ahead along the right-hand field edge to another gate. Continue on into **Upton Lovell**.

④ At a crossroads, take the signed footpath right, then just before the drive to **Hatch House**, follow the path left to a footbridge over the river. Go through a gate and proceed ahead along the field edge to a metal gate. Cross the stile on your left, walk along the hedged

---

path and cross the railway with great care via gates and steps. Continue to a lane in **Corton**.

⑤ Turn left through the village, eventually passing the **Dove Inn**. At the T-junction, take the arrowed path across the stile on your right. Head across the field on a defined path to a stile and keep ahead along the fenced path to a further stile and proceed along the right-hand edge of the field. Shortly, climb a stile and turn left along the field edge to a stile and soon pass beneath the railway.

⑥ Cross a footbridge and then a stile and walk beside the right-hand fence to a gate. From here, follow the grassy track ahead. Cross another stile and keep to the track until you reach a lane. Turn right and follow it through the complex of buildings at **Mill Farm** and across the river to rejoin your outward route beside the River Wylye back into **Heytesbury**.

Wylye Valley Villages

A longer loop takes you to Sherrington and across breezy downland.
See map and information panel for Walk 28

•DISTANCE•	8½ miles (13.7km)
•MINIMUM TIME•	4hrs
•ASCENT / GRADIENT•	360ft (110m) ▲▲▲
•LEVEL OF DIFFICULTY•	🚶 🚶 🚶

Walk 29 Directions (Walk 28 option)

At the crossroads, Point ④, keep straight on to the church and then follow the path ahead to a drive. Turn left, then left again at the lane, soon to bear off right at the bend on to a bridleway. Enter a field and keep right along the edge to the corner. Keep ahead along a straight path through a tunnel of trees to a field. Proceed straight across towards a bungalow, crossing two stiles to a lane, Point Ⓐ. Turn right and continue across the railway and the River Wylye into **Boyton**.

Don't miss St Mary's Church in Boyton, approached along an elegant driveway that also leads to the handsome 17th-century manor house. Inside, the Gifford Chapel has a great wheel window. Pevsner described it as 'a tour-de-force'.

At the junction, turn right, then left in 150yds (137m) to visit Boyton church. Otherwise turn left, pass **Rectory Cottage** then, at a right-hand bend, cross the stile ahead and turn left around the edge of two fields to a stile. Continue to a gate and turn right on a drive. Bear left into **Sherrington**, Point Ⓑ.

Unusually dedicated to two Middle Eastern saints, Damien and Cosmos, the little church possesses some 14th-century glass and an almost complete set of wall-texts used for religious education purposes during the Elizabethan and Jacobean periods.

Turn right through the village, passing the pond, and turn left at the T-junction. In 100yds (91m), cross the stile on the right and walk up the left-hand field edge to a stile. Turn right and soon bear diagonally left uphill to stile. Continue to a further stile and turn right along the track, Point Ⓒ.

Look back across the valley to view the Rising Sun Badge etched into Lamb Down. At 175ft (53m) by 150ft (45m) tall it is a version of the badge used by Anzac troops and was cut out by Australians stationed at Codford in 1916.

Gradually ascend, keep right on merging with a farm road and continue for 1¾ miles (2.8km) to reach a crossing of routes, Point Ⓓ. Turn right, then almost immediately bear left down a bridle path into **Corton**. Cross the lane and descend to the lane opposite the **Dove Inn**. Turn left and join Walk 28 just after Point ⑤.

Walk 30

Devizes and Caen Hill Locks

A stroll around historic streets and Rennie's famous flight of locks.

•DISTANCE•	4¼ miles (6.8km)
•MINIMUM TIME•	2hrs
•ASCENT / GRADIENT•	180ft (55m) ▲ ▲ ▲
•LEVEL OF DIFFICULTY•	🚶🚶 🚶 🚶
•PATHS•	Pavements, canal tow path
•LANDSCAPE•	Town streets and canal
•SUGGESTED MAP•	aqua3 OS Explorers 157 Marlborough & Savernake Forest; 156 Chippenham & Bradford-on-Avon
•START / FINISH•	Grid reference: SU 004617
•DOG FRIENDLINESS•	Dogs can be off lead along tow path
•PARKING•	Devizes Wharf car park
•PUBLIC TOILETS•	Devizes Wharf

Walk 30 Directions

Devizes is Wiltshire's principal market town and takes its name from the Latin *ad divisas* (at the boundaries), as this old town is at the point where the manors of Rowde, Cannings and Potterne once met. The town grew up around the castle, built by Bishop Osmund of Salisbury in 1080. It burnt down and was rebuilt in 1138 by Bishop Roger of Salisbury, builder of Old Sarum and Malmesbury Castle. It was demolished by Cromwell's forces shortly after the Battle of Devizes in 1645 and the present-day building is a Victorian folly.

Devizes has held a market since receiving its first Charter in 1141, so following the demise of the castle, the large market-place became the focal point and the town prospered on the wool trade and dairy produce from the Vale of Pewsey. In the early 19th century, Devizes held the largest corn market in the west of England and also traded in hops,

cattle, horses and cloth. The wool trade's prosperity is mirrored in the wool merchants' 18th-century town houses in St John's and Long Street, and around the fine market-place. Interestingly, the pattern of streets originates from when the first castle was built and survives virtually intact. Other notable buildings to seek out are the Elizabethan timber-framed houses in St John's Alley, Great Porch House in Monday Market Street, probably the oldest surviving building in the town, the 16th-century Bear Hotel, one of a number of historic inns built when

---

WHERE TO EAT AND DRINK

Among the many pubs in Devizes, most serving Wadworth beers, try the friendly **Bear Hotel**, the **Elm Tree** in Long Street, and the **Castle Hotel** in New Park Street. The **Natural Food Café** above the Healthy Life food shop (off Market Place) is good for coffee and light lunches. In summer, refreshments are available at the small café above Caen Hill Locks. Just outside Devizes, at Rowde, visit the **George and Dragon** for innovative pub food, especially fresh fish dishes.

WHAT TO LOOK FOR ℹ

As you stroll through the streets, one of the delights of the town to watch for is the regular delivery of the local brew, Wadworth's, by a **brewer's dray**, pulled by magnificent pair of Shire horses.

Devizes was a major coaching stop, and the two fine Norman churches. Filling the air with the aroma of malt and hops is Wadworth's Brewery, a red brick Victorian building dominating the northern end of the Market Place. To learn more about the town's history, pick up the Town Trail leaflet from the tourist information centre.

From the car park, walk back down **Wharf Street** and turn left along **New Park Street**, passing 18th-century Brownston House and St Mary's Church. At the roundabout, cross the road and walk down **Monday Market Street**, passing between the White Bear and Great Porch House. At a crossroads, keep ahead along **Sheep Street** and then **Bridewell Street** to reach **Long Street**. Turn right, pass the Wiltshire Heritage Museum, St John's Church and the Town Hall to enter the **Market Place**. Pop into the Devizes Visitor Centre, then continue along **Northgate Street**, keeping ahead at the roundabout by Wadworth's Brewery. At the canal bridge, take the path right, signed 'Caen Hill Locks via subway', and join the tow path. Pass under the road and head west to reach the **A361**. Cross over and follow the tow path to **Caen Hill Locks**.

This famous flight is one of the great wonders of the canal era. Completed by John Rennie in 1810, in order to carry the Kennet and Avon Canal to a height of 237ft (72m), the flight consists of 29 locks in all, extending over 2 miles (3.2km). In the early days, the canal was so busy that gas lighting was installed so that boats could negotiate the locks day and night.

Marvel at this amazing feat of engineering as you descend past the locks and large side pounds. At the bottom, turn round and retrace your steps back uphill, possibly pausing at the tea room across the bridge by **Queen Elizabeth II Lock**. Recross the **A361** and walk back to the subway, leaving the tow path to cross the road bridge and join the northern bank of the canal. Follow the tow path to the next bridge, cross it and turn right to pass the Kennet and Avon Canal Museum at **Devizes Wharf**.

The canalside at Devizes Wharf has been revitalised in recent years. Signs of industry have gone and today a stroll along the tow path reveals a pleasant scene, enhanced by the former timbered and balconied granary, built in 1810, which is now the headquarters of the Kennet and Avon Canal Trust and houses a small canal museum. The warehouse, now occupied by the Wharf Theatre, was equipped with a huge crane that could unload goods straight into the building from the boats.

WHILE YOU'RE THERE ℹ

View an interactive exhibition on the medieval origins of Devizes at the **visitor centre** in the Market Place. Allow some time to visit the excellent **Wiltshire Heritage Museum** in Long Street, which boasts one of the finest prehistoric collections in Europe, tracing the history of Wiltshire and its people from the earliest times to the present day through a series of fascinating galleries.

East Knoyle – Wren's Birthplace

Savour wonderful views across the Blackmore Vale on this undulating rural ramble around East Knoyle, birthplace of architect Sir Christopher Wren.

•DISTANCE•	5 miles (8km)
•MINIMUM TIME•	2hrs 30min
•ASCENT / GRADIENT•	590ft (180m) ▲▲▲
•LEVEL OF DIFFICULTY•	👣👣 👣👣 👣
•PATHS•	Field paths, woodland bridle paths, metalled lanes
•LANDSCAPE•	Wooded hillside, undulating farmland, village streets
•SUGGESTED MAP•	aqua3 OS Explorer 143 Warminster & Trowbridge
•START / FINISH•	Grid reference: ST 879305
•DOG FRIENDLINESS•	Can be off lead through woodland and on Windmill Hill
•PARKING•	East Knoyle village hall, adjacent to church
•PUBLIC TOILETS•	None on route

BACKGROUND TO THE WALK

Sleepy East Knoyle clings to the slopes of a greensand ridge on the northern flanks of the Nadder Valley. Comprising of four distinct hamlets – Underhill, Milton, Upton and The Green – it is an appealing scattered parish characterised by charming stone-built cottages and a myriad of tiny lanes that meet close to Windmill Hill, which at 650ft (198m) offers unrivalled views across the Blackmore Vale into deepest Dorset. This is fine walking country and your rural ramble explores the peaceful paths that link the hamlets. It loops round to West Knoyle in the Sem Valley, before ascending Windmill Hill from where, if you time it right, you'll see a magical sunset over the Blackmore Vale.

The Wren Connection

The heart of the village is Underhill where you will find the post office stores, the ancient Church of St Mary the Virigin, and several reminders that East Knoyle was the birthplace of one of Britain's greatest architects, Sir Christopher Wren. His father, Dr Christopher Wren, was appointed rector of East Knoyle in 1623 and married the daughter of a local squire. The rectory in which they lived now forms part of Knoyle Place, an elegant Georgian house built in 1799. Due to a fire at the rectory, their son Christopher was born on 20 October 1632 in a cottage at the bottom of Wise Lane, opposite the present village shop, Wren's Shop. This building was demolished in 1878. Wren's interests lay in mathematics and architecture and his greatest opportunity in the latter came with the rebuilding that followed the London fire of 1666. He re-planned the entire city and supervised the rebuilding of 51 churches, his most famous design being that of St Paul's Cathedral. A stone tablet opposite Wren's Shop records that Wren 'Architect, Mathematician, Patriot' was born in the village.

Knoyle Church and Rector Wren

The most visible reminder of the Wren family can be seen in the church. Pevsner said that every Wiltshire tourist should make a point of seeing this late 13th-century church, notably the chancel which he describes as 'Norman in its bones'. What really makes it interesting are the intricate plaster wall decorations. Designed by Wren's father in 1639, they are unique in an English parish church. Surprisingly, the decorations brought Dr Wren, an ardent Royalist, plenty of trouble during the Civil War. It is said that Roundheads interrupted him working on the plasterwork and thinking he was occupied on idolatrous Papist works of art, they removed him by force and damaged many of the decorations. Although later allowed to continue, he was brought to trial in 1647 accused of 'heretical practices', but doubtless, his real crime was that of being a Royalist. Although the charge of heresy was not sustained, he was fined £40 and his living sequestrated. It is said he returned to East Knoyle and became schoolmaster for five years.

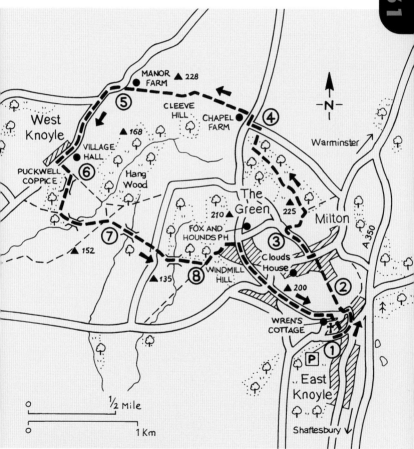

Walk 31 Directions

① Turn left out of the car park into the village. Turn left up **Wise Lane**. Bear left and take the drive right. Keep ahead along the grass track where the drive veers left.

② Keep ahead uphill, soon to bear left along a metalled drive. On reaching the stable buildings of **Clouds House**, take the unmarked path to the right, downhill, passing a garage to reach the lane in **Milton**. Cross over and bear left along the lower lane.

Walk 31

③ Pass a thatched cottage on your right then climb the bank to a stile. Turn right behind a cottage to a gate and climb through the edge of woodland. At the top, bear half-left along the woodland path and soon descend to a bridle path. Turn left, then right at the next junction and follow the woodland path downhill to a lane.

④ Turn left, then right at the T-junction. Take the bridle path left beyond **Chapel Farm**, immediately forking right along a track to a gate. Continue along the field edge, following it left to a gate in the field corner. Gradually descend off **Cleeve Hill**, passing through two gates and **Manor Farm** to the lane in **West Knoyle**.

> ### WHILE YOU'RE THERE
> Nine miles (14.5km) west along the A303 is **Stourhead**, one of the National Trust's finest gardens. Designed by Henry Hoare II and laid out between 1741 and 1780, it is an outstanding example of an English landscaped garden, with classical temples set around a lake, and magnificent woodland with exotic trees. Also, view a Palladian mansion and enjoy estate walks (► Walks 43 and 44).

⑤ Keep ahead and continue through the village for ½ mile (800m). Pass the village hall, then just beyond the 'The Willows', turn left to a gate beside **Puckwell Coppice**. Follow the track ahead to an information board. Take the permissive footpath to the right, through a gate.

⑥ Proceed ahead, cross a footbridge and keep right at the fork of paths. Shortly, bear left with the footpath that exits the wood to your right and descend through trees to a footbridge. Bear left and

> ### WHAT TO LOOK FOR
> Note the elegant and appropriately named hilltop mansion, **Clouds**, as you ascend towards Milton. It was built for the Wyndham family by Philip Webb in 1886 at the cost of £80,000, but had to be rebuilt in 1891 at a further cost of £35,000 after a fire.

follow the grassy swathe to a gap in the field corner. Continue ahead, then turn right along the first grassy swathe to a gate.

⑦ Bear slightly right to a kissing gate, cross a footbridge and keep straight on to a fence stile. Turn right along the track, then left through a gate and bear diagonally right, soon to descend to a fence stile and copse. Cross a footbridge and the wire fence and keep straight ahead, uphill through the trees to enter a field. Continue beside woodland to a gate in the top left-hand corner.

⑧ Follow the bridleway uphill through woodland. At a junction, turn left, then at the top, bear right into a cul-de-sac to reach the lane. Turn left for the **Fox and Hounds**. Turn right to reach **Windmill Hill**, keep ahead at crossroads and descend into **East Knoyle**. Take the metalled footpath beside **Wren's Cottage**, cross a lane and descend steps into the churchyard. At the road, turn right to get back to the car park.

> ### WHERE TO EAT AND DRINK
> The creeper-covered **Seymour Arms** in the village centre offers generous home-cooked food and Wadworth ales. A short diversion at Windmill Hill will bring you to the **Fox & Hounds** at The Green. Enjoy hearty pub meals, a good range of beers in the rambling bars and great views from the garden.

Fonthill's Fantastic Folly

Learn about Fonthill's eccentric 18th-century owner, William Beckford, and his grand Gothic folly on this delightful walk across elegant parkland.

•DISTANCE•	4¼ miles (6.8km)
•MINIMUM TIME•	2hrs
•ASCENT / GRADIENT•	278ft (85m) ▲▲▲
•LEVEL OF DIFFICULTY•	🏃🏃 🏃🏃 🏃🏃
•PATHS•	Tracks, field and woodland paths, parkland, some road walking
•LANDSCAPE•	Wooded hillside, rolling parkland
•SUGGESTED MAP•	aqua3 OS Explorer 143 Warminster & Trowbridge
•START / FINISH•	Grid reference: ST 933316
•DOG FRIENDLINESS•	Keep dogs under control at all times
•PARKING•	Lay-by close to southern end of Fonthill Lake
•PUBLIC TOILETS•	None on route

BACKGROUND TO THE WALK

The vast Fonthill Estate lies tucked away on the rolling northern flanks of the unspoilt Nadder Valley between Tisbury, one of Wiltshire's oldest small towns, and the charming village of Hindon. This wonderful short walk explores Fonthill Park, with its beautiful tree-fringed lake and splendid triumphal-style gateway, attributed to Inigo Jones, and ridge-top woodland and pastures between the estate villages of Fonthill Bishop and Fonthill Gifford. Fonthill House lies secluded on a wooded hillside above the sweeping parkland and to the casual passer-by it is the epitomy of a perfect country estate. It is also the setting for the most fantastic story to be found in Wiltshire.

Fonthill's Eccentric Owner

Fonthill Estate was acquired by William Beckford, a Lord Mayor of London in the mid-18th century. Having built the Palladian mansion, Fonthill Splendens, he died in 1770 leaving a large fortune from sugar plantations to his ten-year-old son William. An utterly spoilt, capricious and extravagant child, England's richest young man embraced Romanticism in all its form, travelling across Europe and writing weird and fantastic tales, notably *Vathek*, a seminal Gothic novel about a hero who lived alone in a mighty tower. Unlike other Romantic writers, the eccentric Beckford had the means to indulge his fantasies.

Beckford's Great Gothic Folly

Beckford surrounded his estate with a 12 mile (19.3km) long and 12 ft (3.6m) high wall, and commisioned James Wyatt in 1796 to build his Gothic dream palace, a grandiose, partly ruined 'abbey', deep in woodland to the west of Fonthill Lake. Beckford and the slapdash Wyatt built in a great hurry, employing 500 men to work day and night and kept fires burning to prevent plaster and cement from freezing. By 1800, the cruciform building had a central tower 275ft (84m) high and, although unfinished, work had progressed enough for Beckford to entertain Nelson and Lady Hamilton here. Although never completed, the scale of the plan for the abbey was such that the tower was intended to have a spire, elevating it to 450ft (137m), overtopping Salisbury Cathedral by 50ft (15m). Beckford finally moved into the abbey in 1807.

For the next 15 years he lived in the unfinished building as a recluse then, in 1823 when his funds had virtually run dry, he sold the estate to John Farquhar, an equally eccentric gunpowder millionaire, and moved to Bath. Two years later, owing to Wyatt's negligence and dishonest builders, the massive foundationless tower collapsed in a storm, bringing down much of the rest of the abbey. Beckford, meanwhile, was busy building an Italianate tower on the top of Lansdown Hill. Fortunately this didn't collapse and is now the finest surviving example of his work. Fonthill was the classic folly, 'the most prodigious romantic folly in England' as Pevsner described it. Sadly, you are unable to see the abbey remains, a small turret room and the battlemented cloisters, as they are incorporated into a house at the end of a private drive.

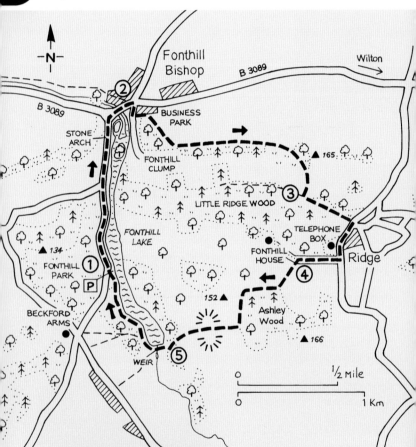

Walk 32 Directions

① With your back to the lay-by, turn right along the road (this can be busy) that traverses **Fonthill**

Park beside the lake for just over ½ mile (800m). Pass beneath the magnificent stone arch and shortly bear right to the **B3089**. Keep to the right along the pavement into the pretty village of **Fonthill Bishop**.

Walk 32

WHAT TO LOOK FOR

Only a wing (a pair of cottages) of **Fonthill Splendens** remains beside the present Fonthill House. The rest was pulled down by Beckford before he decided to build his Gothic fantasy elsewhere on the estate. Take a closer look at **Fonthill Lake**. It was used as a location for the filming of Joanne Harris' novel, *Chocolat*, when a mock galleon was deliberately blown up here.

② Turn right just beyond the bus shelter on to a metalled track. On passing the 'Private Road' sign for Fonthill Estate, turn left through a small business park on an unsigned footpath. Keep left and soon join a track that bears right uphill towards woodland. Follow the grassy track beside **Fonthill Clump** and keep to the main track above the valley. In ½ mile (800m) bear right downhill into **Little Ridge Wood**.

③ The track gives way to a path. At a T-junction, bear left and keep left at the next two junctions, following the wide path to a gate and lane. Turn right through the hamlet of

Ridge. Pass the telephone box, walk uphill and bear off right with yellow arrow along the drive to **Fonthill House**.

④ In ¼ mile (400m), fork left with the footpath sign to follow a track beside paddocks to pass beside a gate. In 20yds (18m) fork right with a yellow arrow and walk beside woodland. On entering an open field, turn left along the field edge, the path becoming a defined grassy track around the field edge. With good views, gradually descend towards woodland.

WHERE TO EAT AND DRINK

Drive south from the lay-by for ½ mile (800m) to reach the excellent **Beckford Arms**. Expect log fires, tasteful decor throughout, rambling bars, a relaxed atmosphere, interesting food from ciabatta sandwiches to rack of lamb, local ales and a sun-trap patio and garden. Alternatively, try the **Angel** or the **Lamb** in Hindon.

⑤ Enter the wood and bear left then right along a gravel track beside **Fonthill Lake**. Cross the weir to a gate. Disregard the track which goes ahead uphill and bear off right along the lakeside edge. Follow the well established path through two gates, eventually returning to the parking area.

WHILE YOU'RE THERE

Enjoy a stroll around **Hindon**, 2 miles (3.2km) north. Founded by the Bishops of Winchester between 1220 and 1250 and handsomely rebuilt by Wyatt following a fire in 1754, it has a wide attractive High Street lined with stone cottages and two fine inns. Visit Tisbury to see the largest medieval **tithe barn** in England, situated amidst a fine collection of 14th- and 15th-century buildings at Place Farm.

Walk 33

Tollard Royal and General Pitt-Rivers

A walk around Rushmore Park in the heart of Cranborne Chase.

•DISTANCE•	4½ miles (7.2km)
•MINIMUM TIME•	2hrs
•ASCENT / GRADIENT•	616ft (188m) ▲▲▲
•LEVEL OF DIFFICULTY•	🚶 🚶 🚶
•PATHS•	Field and woodland paths, bridle paths and tracks
•LANDSCAPE•	Chalk downland, sheltered combes, woodland
•SUGGESTED MAP•	aqua3 OS Explorer 118 Shaftesbury & Cranborne Chase
•START / FINISH•	Grid reference: ST 944178
•DOG FRIENDLINESS•	Can be off lead along Ox Drove and on Win Green Hill
•PARKING•	By pond in Tollard Royal
•PUBLIC TOILETS•	None on route

BACKGROUND TO THE WALK

Bordering on Dorset, this tranquil corner of south Wiltshire lies in the heart of Cranborne Chase, an undulating tract of chalk downland with breezy ridges and secluded dry valleys or 'bottoms' – one of which hides the village of Tollard Royal. This spectacular walk leads you around the rolling parkland of the Rushmore Estate, formerly the home of the 19th-century archaeologist and ethnologist General Pitt-Rivers, and offers you the option to ascend Win Green Hill, one of the highest points in Wiltshire at 911ft (277m).

Tangled copses and a belt of woodland are all that remain of the great forest that covered an area of some 90 miles (145km). The oldest part, with hunting rights dating back to the time of King John (1167–1216), is centred around Tollard Royal. John hunted on the Chase and owned a small estate at Tollard, hence the 'Royal' in the village name. His lodge was on the site now occupied by King John's House, an elegant Elizabethan manor house near the church. By the 18th century, the forest had become a refuge for poachers, smugglers and vagabonds, and violent, often murderous, disputes arose continually between them and the keepers of the forest. After hunting rights ended in 1828, Lord Rivers destroyed much of the ancient forest, reducing it to more manageable proportions.

Often referred to as the 'father of English archaeology', General Augustus Pitt-Rivers (1827–1900) inherited the Rushmore Estate in 1880. Winning his rank during the Crimean War, he found fame as a scientist and archaeologist through excavating earthworks, building up collections and turning to ethnological artefacts to demonstrate his theories of cultural evolution. He devoted the last 20 years of his life to excavating archaeological sites on the estate, resulting in five volumes of notes and sketches. He built a private museum in Farnham, 3 miles (4.8km) away, to house his models and local collections. This closed in the 1960s and most of the exhibits went to Oxford University, although you can see scale models, drawings and artefacts in the Salisbury and South Wiltshire Museum in Salisbury.

Pitt-Rivers died at Rushmore in 1900 and you will find a memorial to the family in the church of St Peter ad Vincula Church in Tollard Royal. As you skirt Rushmore Park on your walk, you will glimpse his former home, Rushmore Lodge, through the trees.

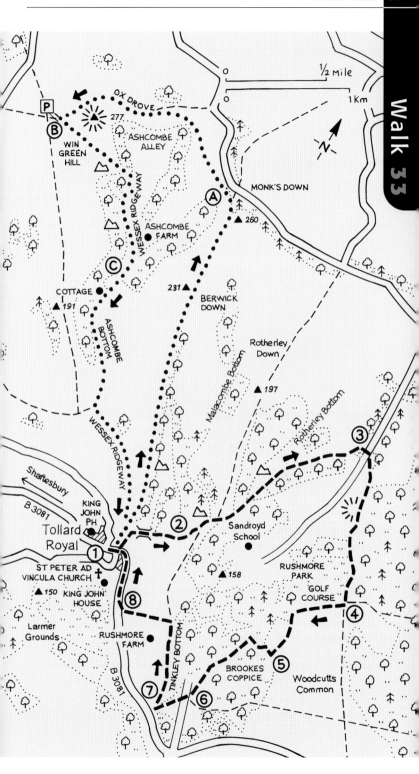

½ mile
1 Km

OX DROVE

P

B

WIN
GREEN
HILL

▲ 277

ASHCOMBE
ALLEY

N

MONK'S DOWN

Ⓐ

WESSEX RIDGEWAY

ASHCOMBE
FARM

▲ 260

COTTAGE

Ⓒ

▲ 191

231 ▲

BERWICK
DOWN

ASHCOMBE BOTTOM

Rotherley
Down

Malacombe Bottom

▲ 197

Rotherley Bottom

Ⓑ

WESSEX RIDGEWAY

③

Shaftesbury

B 3081

KING
JOHN PH

②

Sandroyd
School

Tollard
Royal

①

ST PETER AD
VINCULA CHURCH

▲ 150   KING JOHN
HOUSE

⑧

RUSHMORE
PARK

GOLF
COURSE

④

▲ 158

Larmer
Grounds

RUSHMORE
FARM

TINKLEY BOTTOM

BROOKES
COPPICE

⑤

Woodcutts
Common

B 3081

⑦

⑥

Walk 33 Directions

① Facing the pond turn left along the metalled track and take the waymarked path right across the footbridge to a stile. Follow the narrow path half-left uphill through scrub and along the field edge, soon to bear right to a gate in the top corner. Keep ahead, pass to the right of a copse and bear left through gates into the adjacent field. Keep to the right-hand edge, downhill to a gate and stile.

② Bear diagonally left and steeply descend to a gate and junction of paths in the valley bottom. Take the track right, through a gate and continue to a fork of tracks. Steeply ascend the grassy track ahead and follow it beside woodland for ½ mile (800m). Bear right through trees to a metalled lane.

> **WHERE TO EAT AND DRINK** ⓘ
> Seek rest and refreshment at the **King John** pub in Tollard Royal before tackling the energetic longer loop, Walk 34. Teas are available at **Larmer Tree Gardens** for those visiting them.

③ Turn right, then left before the gates to **Rushmore Park**. Keep to the established track, with cameo views across the park, heading gently downhill to a crossing of paths by the **golf course**.

④ Turn right, pass in front of a cottage and keep to the path

> **WHILE YOU'RE THERE** ⓘ
> Visit **Larmer Tree Gardens** just off the A354 south of Tollard Royal. Created in 1880 by General Pitt-Rivers they contain a collection of Colonial and Oriental buildings, a Roman temple and an open-air theatre.

through rough grass alongside the fairway. Bear right on to a track and follow it left to reach redundant gate posts. Pass beside the gate posts and follow the track right. Where this peters out, keep ahead beside woodland, bearing right to pass a green on your left.

⑤ Bear right through a gate into the woodland and follow the yellow waymarker sharp right through the trees. At first ill-defined, the path soon bears left to become a clear route (yellow arrows) through **Brookes Coppice**, to reach a T-junction with a track.

⑥ Turn left, cross the drive and stile opposite and bear half-right across parkland to a stile beyond an avenue of trees. Bear slightly left downhill to a gate in the field corner. In a few paces take the second arrowed path sharp right.

⑦ Follow the track through **Tinkley Bottom** to a gate and pass below **Rushmore Farm**. On passing through the second of two gateways, turn immediately left and walk uphill to a pair of gates. Go through the left-hand gate and keep right through two paddocks to reach a gate.

⑧ Take the path ahead and bear diagonally right downhill to a gate and the **B3081**. Keep ahead into **Tollard Royal** back to the pond and your car.

> **WHAT TO LOOK FOR** ⓘ
> In the nave of **St Peter ad Vincula Church** (St Peter in Chains) in Tollard Royal you will see a 14th-century cross-legged effigy of Sir William Payne who died in 1388. The armour is of banded mail, a rare example found on only four other effigies in England.

To a Wiltshire High Point

A longer loop takes in Win Green Hill and some memorable views.
See map and information panel for Walk 33

•DISTANCE•	5½ miles (8.8km)
•MINIMUM TIME•	2hrs 30min
•ASCENT / GRADIENT•	541ft (165m) ▲▲▲
•LEVEL OF DIFFICULTY•	👥 👥 👥

Walk 34 Directions (Walk 33 option)

Walk along the metalled track, disregard the path taken on Walk 33, then bear right at a fork along the signed '**Byway to Win Green**' and steeply ascend the stony track. Remain on this established track as it steadily climbs to the top of **Berwick Down**. Continue to climb, the track curving left to reach a junction of ways at the summit of **Monk's Down**, Point Ⓐ. Ignore the metalled track on your right and proceed ahead, keeping right at the fork to follow the ancient **Ox Drove** track along the top of the chalk downland.

Stay on this lofty track around the top of the **Ashcombe Valley** and soon reach **Win Green Hill**. Ascend the track to the car park. Turn left through the car park, Point Ⓑ and keep right to join the grassy path close to the right-hand fence. You can also bear left here to the summit of Win Green Hill.

Owned by the National Trust, Win Green Hill is characterised by a steep scarp face and long sweeping slopes, the chalk supporting a rich variety of plant species, including the burnt orchid, round-headed campion and yellow-wort.

Shortly, cross a stile on your right to join the **Wessex Ridgeway**. Disregard the swing gate on the right and bear left along the field edge. Follow marker posts steeply downhill through grassland to reach a gate within woodland. Continue straight on and soon bear right along a track on emerging from the trees. Descend steeply and soon merge with the track through **Ashcombe Bottom**. Keep right and pass **Ashcombe Farm**.

In 1930 the photographer, designer, painter and writer Sir Cecil Beaton (1904–80) rented Ashcombe House. He is buried in Broad Chalke in the neighbouring Ebble Valley.

Where the track bears right uphill, Point Ⓒ, keep straight on and follow the path to the right of a gate and track. Pass in front of a cottage and continue through rough scrub to a stile. Bear left to join the track and continue through the valley bottom. Just before reaching a gate, bear off left to cross a waymarked stile. Bear half-left to a further stile and turn left to a gate. Continue along the grassy track to a gate and follow the track back to the pond in the village centre.

The Battle on Roundway Hill

Explore the breezy site of a famous Civil War battle and the ramparts of an Iron-Age hill fort.

•DISTANCE•	4½ miles (7.2km)
•MINIMUM TIME•	2hrs
•ASCENT / GRADIENT•	262ft (80m) ▲▲▲
•LEVEL OF DIFFICULTY•	🚶🚶 🚶🚶 🚶🚶
•PATHS•	Tracks, field paths, stretches of road, 1 stile
•LANDSCAPE•	High chalk downland
•SUGGESTED MAP•	aqua3 OS Explorer 157 Marlborough & Savernake Forest
•START / FINISH•	Grid reference: SU 013639
•DOG FRIENDLINESS•	Can be off lead along tracks but under control on farmland
•PARKING•	Car park by The Plantation north of Roundway village
•PUBLIC TOILETS•	None on route

Walk 35 **Directions**

Roundway Hill forms a wide ridge of high chalk downland below the summits of Beacon Hill, King's Play Hill and Morgan's Hill, which rise steeply out of the Avon Valley north of Devizes. Now a peaceful scene of wide open fields and grassy scarp slopes affording fine views towards the Cotswolds and Salisbury Plain, this breezy, unspoilt downland once rang with the sound of battle cries. On 13 July 1643 a small Royalist army defeated the Parliamentarians in a bloody skirmish that killed over 600 troops and saw 1,200 wounded or captured.

It was following an indecisive battle at Lansdown near Bath that the Parliamentarian army, led by Sir William Waller, pursued a weakened Royalist army and their blinded leader Lord Hopton to Devizes where they had occupied the castle and barricaded the streets. Weary, short of ammunition and aware that an unfortified Devizes would

not withstand a siege for long, Hopton sent Prince Maurice to Oxford for reinforcements. Knowing that Hopton's cavalry were in bad shape, yet unaware that Prince Maurice had escaped from the town, Waller took his time in besieging the town as his troops needed rest following the Battle of Lansdown. Eventually, news that Prince Maurice and Lord Wilmot were returning to Devizes with three brigades of cavalry (2,000 men), forced Waller to rally his troops on Roundway Down.

From the parking area take the track on your left which leads you across **Roundway Hill** for 1¼ miles (2km). Initially well surfaced, it

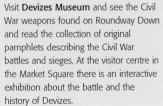

WHILE YOU'RE THERE
Visit **Devizes Museum** and see the Civil War weapons found on Roundway Down and read the collection of original pamphlets describing the Civil War battles and sieges. At the visitor centre in the Market Square there is an interactive exhibition about the battle and the history of Devizes.

Walk 35

becomes grassier and rutted as it swings slightly left to pass the site of the Civil War battle.

Waller sent out his cavalry, known as 'The Lobsters', to meet Wilmot's brigade and it was here that the two mounted armies clashed. Wilmot's troopers charged twice and forced the Parliamentarians west towards Oliver's Castle. Waller's infantry was unable to fire at the Royalists for fear of hitting their own men.

At a crossing of tracks, turn left along a gravelled track. On passing a barn the track becomes metalled, then in ½ mile (800m), at **Hill Cottage**, fork left. Where the track swings left, keep straight on along a narrow, rutted and often muddy track. Gently ascend and near the summit, climb the stepped stile on your left and keep straight ahead between two fields, with excellent views unfolding to your right. In 400yds (366m), turn right and follow the footpath around the top of the escarpment and around **Oliver's Castle**, eventually reaching a gate by a steep combe known as **Bloody Ditch**.

The fleeing Parliamentarian cavalry, unaware of the steep scarp slope on the other side of Oliver's Castle, was chased to the edge and forced down the slope. Many men and horses broke their necks as they plunged over the 300ft (91m) precipice. Others were killed by the newly arrived Royalist infantry who had sallied forth from Devizes on hearing a prearranged gun signal from Lord Wilmot. Since then, this combe has been known as Bloody Ditch and skeletons and military equipment are still occasionally found in the area. Wilmot's cavalry returned to attack Waller's infantry,

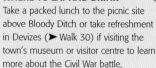

> **WHERE TO EAT AND DRINK** ⓘ
> Take a packed lunch to the picnic site above Bloody Ditch or take refreshment in Devizes (▶ Walk 30) if visiting the town's museum or visitor centre to learn more about the Civil War battle.

who fought on bravely. But, seeing the 2,000 Royalists troops rising over Roundway Down from Devizes, they broke and fled, and many were cut down by the victorious Royalists. The hill was subsequently named Runaway Hill by the Royalists, and this later became Roundway. The defeat of a superior balanced army arrayed in proper battle order by a column of cavalry that had ridden down from Oxford was regarded as a remarkable event. As a result of this loss, Waller was unable to replace the Earl of Wessex as Lord General of the Parliamentary army. Also, with no Parliamentary forces left in the West Country, the Royalists had won an important victory.

Walk beside woodland, cross a stile to a parking area and keep straight on along a track, ignoring a similar track right. In 200yds (183m), where the track swings left, turn right across a stile and walk along the left-hand field edge. Gradually ascend, then in the top corner, turn left over a stile into a wooded enclosure and turn right down the track just within the woodland. At the road, turn left, then left again, uphill to the car park.

> **WHAT TO LOOK FOR** ⓘ
> At the end of the walk, view the newest of the Wiltshire White Horses, the **Millennium White Horse** cut into Roundway Down in late 1999 to replace the White Horse that had long been overgrown since it was first cut in 1845.

Walk 36

A Walk with Good Manors from Holt

A gentle farmland stroll from a rare Wiltshire industrial village leads you to a beautiful 15th-century moated manor house.

•DISTANCE•	3 miles (4.8km)
•MINIMUM TIME•	1hr 30min
•ASCENT / GRADIENT•	147ft (45m) ▲ ▲ ▲
•LEVEL OF DIFFICULTY•	🚶🚶 🚶🚶 🚶🚶
•PATHS•	Field paths, metalled track, country lanes, 8 stiles
•LANDSCAPE•	Gently undulating farmland
•SUGGESTED MAP•	aqua3 OS Explorer 156 Chippenham & Bradford-on-Avon
•START / FINISH•	Grid reference: ST 861619
•DOG FRIENDLINESS•	Keep dogs under control at all times
•PARKING•	Holt Village Hall car park
•PUBLIC TOILETS•	Only if visiting The Courts or Great Chalfield Manor

BACKGROUND TO THE WALK

Threaded by the busy B3107 linking Melksham to Bradford-on-Avon, Holt is a rare industrial Wiltshire village with a significant history as a cloth-making and leather-tanning centre. The tannery, founded in the early 18th century, still occupies the main three-storey factory in the appropriately named small industrial area – The Midlands – while bedding manufacture and light engineering now occupy former cloth factories. Holt also enjoyed short-lived fame between 1690 and 1750 as a spa, based on the curative properties of a spring, but its popularity declined in face of competition from nearby Bath. The most attractive part of the village is at Ham Green where elegant 17th- and 18th-century houses stand along three sides of a fine green shaded by horse chestnut trees, and a quiet lane leads to the late Victorian parish church with a Perpendicular tower.

The Courts – Wiltshire's Secret Garden

From the green a walled walk leads to The Courts, a substantial 18th-century house that served, as its name suggests, as the place where the local magistrate sat to adjudicate in the disputes of the cloth weavers from Bradford-on-Avon. Although not open, the house makes an attractive backdrop to 7 acres (2.8ha) of authentic English country garden owned by the National Trust. Hidden away behind high walls and reached through an avenue of pleached limes, you will find a series of garden 'rooms' that are full of charm and a haven of peace away from the busy village street. Stroll along a network of stone paths through formal gardens featuring yew topiary, lawns with colourful herbaceous borders, a lake and lily pond with aquatic and water-tolerant plants, and explore an area given over to wild flowers among an interesting small arboretum of trees and shrubs.

Great Chalfield Manor

You will glimpse the Tudor chimneys and gabled windows of this enchanting manor house as you stride across peaceful field paths a mile (1.6km) or so north west of Holt. Enhanced by a moat and gatehouse, this exquisite group of buildings will certainly live up to your expectations and really must be visited. Built in 1480, during the Wars of the Roses, by Thomas Tropenell, Great Chalfield is one of the most perfect examples of the late medieval English manor house which, together with its immediately adjacent church, mill, great barn and other Elizabethan farm buildings, makes a harmonious and memorable visual group.

Sensitively restored in the early 20th century by Sir Harold Brakspear after two centuries of neglect and disrepair, the manor house is centred on its traditional great hall, which rises to the rafters and is lit by windows, including two beautiful oriels, positioned high in the walls. Join one of the guided tours and you will be able to see the fine vaulting, the chimney place of the hall, the concealed spy-holes in the gallery, designed to allow people to see what was going on in the great hall, and the amusing ornaments, gargoyles and other fascinating details of this fine building.

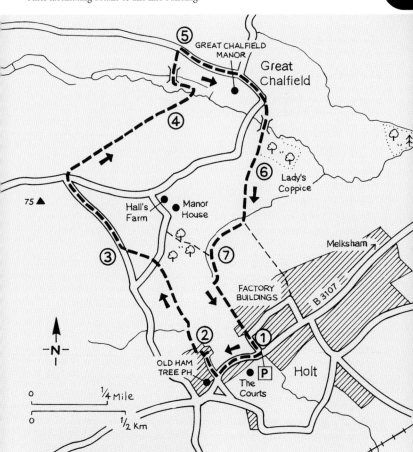

Walk 36 **Directions**

① Turn left out of the car park and then right along the **B3107** through the village. Just before reaching the

Old Ham Tree pub and village green, turn right along **Crown Corner**. At the end of the lane take the waymarked path left along a drive. Follow the fenced path beside 'Highfields' to a stile.

Walk 36

WHERE TO EAT AND DRINK ℹ

You will find a choice of pubs in Holt. The 16th-century **Tollgate Inn** offers innovative, freshly produced food on varied menus alongside fine wines and local ales. For more traditional pub food and atmosphere head for the **Old Ham Tree** which overlooks the green.

② Keep to the right along the edge of the field, then keep ahead in the next field towards the clump of fir trees. Continue following the worn path to the right, into a further field. Keep left along the field edge to a stile in the top corner. Maintain direction to a ladder stile and cross the metalled drive and stile opposite. Bear diagonally left through the field to a hidden stile in the hedge, level with the clump of trees to your right.

③ Turn right along the lane. At a junction, turn right towards **Great Chalfield** and go through the kissing gate almost immediately on your left. Take the arrowed path right, diagonally across a large field towards **Great Chalfield Manor** visible ahead.

④ Cross a stile and bear half-right downhill to a stile. Cross the stream via stepping stones, then a stile and bear diagonally left across the field to a gate. Cross the bridge and keep ahead beside the hedge to a metalled track by a barn.

⑤ Turn right, then right again when you reach the lane, passing in front of **Great Chalfield Manor**. At the sharp right-hand bend, go through the gate ahead and bear right, then half-left across the field to cross a footbridge over a stream. Continue straight on up the field beside woodland to a gate in the field corner.

WHAT TO LOOK FOR ℹ

A huge **factory** dominates the landscape south of Holt, standing beside the River Avon on the site of a 16th-century cloth mill. The present building dates from 1824 and belongs to Nestlé who manufacture processed foods here. All that remains of **Holt Spa** is an arch, pump handle and stone tablet on one of the factory walls in the industrial estate.

⑥ Follow the left-hand field edge to a gate, then follow the path straight ahead towards a chimney on the skyline. Go through a gate, bear immediately right to a gate in the hedge and turn right along the path around the field edge.

⑦ Ignore the stile on your right and continue to the field corner and a raised path beside water. Go through a gate and turn left along the field edge to a further gate on your left. Join the drive past **Garlands Farm** and pass between small factory buildings to the road and turn right back to the car park.

WHILE YOU'RE THERE ℹ

Visit **Trowbridge Museum**, located in the town's last working woollen mill, and learn more about the woollen mills and cloth-making industry of the Avon Valley in West Wiltshire.

Castle Combe and By Brook

*Through the hilly and wooded By Brook Valley from Wiltshire's famous
picture-book village.*

·DISTANCE·	5¾ miles (9.2km)
·MINIMUM TIME·	2hrs 30min
·ASCENT / GRADIENT·	515ft (157m) ▲▲▲
·LEVEL OF DIFFICULTY·	🚶🚶 🚶🚶 🚶🚶
·PATHS·	Field and woodland paths and tracks, metalled lanes, 10 stiles
·LANDSCAPE·	Wooded river valley and village streets
·SUGGESTED MAP·	aqua3 OS Explorer 156 Chippenham & Bradford-on-Avon
·START / FINISH·	Grid reference: ST 845776
·DOG FRIENDLINESS·	Keep under control across pasture and golf course
·PARKING·	Free car park just off B4039 at Upper Castle Combe
·PUBLIC TOILETS·	Castle Combe

BACKGROUND TO THE WALK

To many, the idyllic village of Castle Combe needs no introduction since it has featured on countless calendars, chocolate-box lids and jig-saw puzzles. Since being voted 'the prettiest village in England' in 1962, there have been more visitors to it, more photographs taken of it and more words written about it than any other village in the county. Nestling deep in a steam-threaded combe, just a mile (1.6km), and a world away, from the M4, it certainly has all the elements to make it a tourist's dream. You'll find 15th-century Cotswold stone cottages with steep gabled roofs surrounding a turreted church and stone-canopied market cross, a medieval manor house, a fast-flowing steam in the main street leading to an ancient packhorse bridge and a perfectly picturesque river.

Yet, as preservation is taken so seriously here, a palpable atmosphere of unreality surrounds this tiny 'toytown', where television aerials don't exist, gardens are immaculately kept, and the inevitable commercialism is carefully concealed. Behind this present-day façade, however, exists a fascinating history that's well worth exploring, and the timeless valleys and tumbling wooded hillsides that surround the village are favourite Wiltshire walking destinations. If you don't like crowds and really want to enjoy Castle Combe, undertake this walk on a winter weekday.

'Castlecombe' Cloth

The Castle, which gave the village its name, began life as a Roman fort and was used by the Saxons before becoming a Norman castle in 1135 and the home of the de Dunstanville family. In the 13th and 14th centuries the village established itself as an important weaving centre as Sir John Fastolf, the lord of the manor, erected fulling mills along the By Brook and 50 cottages for his workers. With the growth of the cloth trade in Wiltshire, Castle Combe prospered greatly, becoming more like a town with a weekly market and an annual fair that was regarded as 'The most celebrated faire in North Wiltshire for sheep'.

The greatest tribute to the wealth of the weaving industry is reflected in St Andrew's Church which was enlarged during the 15th century. Its impressive Perpendicular tower was built in 1436. For centuries the villages produced a red and white cloth known as Castlecombe. Cloth manufacture began to decline in the early 18th century when the diminutive By Brook was unable to power the larger machinery being introduced. People moved to the larger towns and Castle Combe became depopulated and returned to an agricultural existence. An annual fair, centred around the Market Cross, continued until 1904, and Castle Combe remained an 'estate' village until 1947 when the whole village was sold at auction.

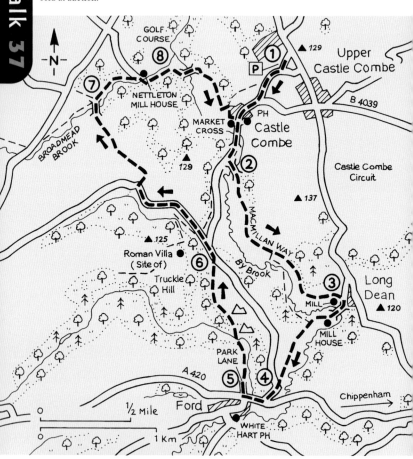

Walk 37 **Directions**

① Leave the car park via the steps and turn right. At the T-junction, turn right and follow the lane into **Castle Combe**. Keep left at the **Market Cross**, cross the **By Brook** and continue along the road to take the path, signed '**Long Dean**', across the second bridge on your left.

② Cross a stile and follow the path uphill and then beside the right-hand fence above the valley (**Macmillan Way**). Beyond an open area, gently ascend through woodland to a stile and gate. Cross a further stile and descend into the hamlet of **Long Dean**.

③ Pass the mill and follow the track right to cross the river bridge.

Walk 37

WHERE TO EAT AND DRINK
The **White Hart** at Ford is the perfect halfway refuelling stop. Expect excellent real ales, interesting bar food and a riverside garden. In Castle Combe, head for the part-timbered 14th-century **White Hart** for cosy log fires, a summer patio garden and an extensive pub menu. Across the road, the more up-market **Castle Inn** offers a more contemporary menu. The impressive **Manor House Hotel** is the place to go for civilised afternoon teas.

At a mill house, keep right and follow the sunken bridleway uphill to a gate. Shortly enter sloping pasture and follow the defined path around the top edge, bearing left to reach a stile and lane.

④ Turn left and descend to the A420 at **Ford**. Turn right along the pavement and shortly turn right again into **Park Lane**. (If you want to visit the White Hart in Ford village, take the road ahead on your left, signed 'Colerne'.) Climb the gravel track and take the footpath left through a squeeze stile.

⑤ Keep right through pasture and continue through trees to a water-meadow in the valley bottom. Turn left, cross a stream and steeply ascend the grassy slope ahead of you, bearing left beyond some trees towards a waymarker post. Follow the footpath along the top of the field to a stile and gate, then walk through the woodland to a gate and the road.

⑥ Turn left, then immediately left again, signed 'North Wraxall'. Keep to the road for ¼ mile (400m) and take the arrowed bridleway right. Follow the track then, just before a gate, keep right downhill on a sunken path to a footbridge over **Broadmead Brook**.

⑦ In 20yds (18m), climb the stile on your right and follow the footpath close to the river. Cross a stile and soon pass beside **Nettleton Mill House**, bearing right to a hidden gate. Walk beside the stream, cross a stile and you will soon reach the golf course.

⑧ Turn right along the metalled track, cross the bridge and turn immediately right again. At a gate, follow the path left below the golf course fairway. Walk beside a wall to reach a stile on your right. Drop down steps to a metalled drive and keep ahead back into **Castle Combe**. Turn left at the **Market Cross** and retrace steps.

WHILE YOU'RE THERE
Linger by the **bridge** over the By Brook and recall, if you've seen it, the 1966 film *Dr Doolittle* starring Rex Harrison. Although miles from the nearest coast, a jetty was built on the banks in front of the 17th-century cottages here to create a fishing harbour, complete with seven boats and plastic cobbles. Local people became 'extras' at £2 10s per day, with meals, alcohol and clothes all thrown in. The film put Castle Combe firmly on the tourist map!

WHAT TO LOOK FOR
St Andrew's Church, in Castle Combe, is worth closer inspection. On the parapet, note the 50 stone heads and the carving of a shuttle and scissors, the mark of the cloth industry put there by merchants who built the church. Inside, don't miss the rare faceless clock made by a local blacksmith in 1380, and the 13th-century tomb of Sir Walter de Dunstanville. Along the By Brook, note the former **fulling mills** and **weavers' cottages** at the remote and unspoilt hamlet of Long Dean.

Lacock – the Birthplace of Photography

Combine a stroll around England's finest medieval village with a riverside walk and a visit to Lacock Abbey, home of photographic pioneer Fox Talbot.

•DISTANCE•	2 miles (3.2km)
•MINIMUM TIME•	1hr
•ASCENT / GRADIENT•	16ft (5m) ▲ ▲ ▲
•LEVEL OF DIFFICULTY•	🚶 🚶 🚶
•PATHS•	Field paths and tracks; some road walking, 6 stiles
•LANDSCAPE•	River valley
•SUGGESTED MAP•	aqua3 OS Explorer 156 Chippenham & Bradford-on-Avon
•START / FINISH•	Grid reference: ST 918681
•DOG FRIENDLINESS•	Dogs can be off lead on riverside pastures if free of cattle
•PARKING•	Free car park on edge of Lacock
•PUBLIC TOILETS•	Adjacent to Stables Tea Room in Lacock village

BACKGROUND TO THE WALK

Timeless Lacock could stand as the pattern of the perfect English village with its twisting streets, packed with attractive buildings from the 15th to 18th centuries, possessing all the character and atmosphere of medieval England. Half-timbering, lichen grey stone, red brick and whitewashed façades crowd together and above eye-level, uneven upper storeys, gabled ends and stone roofs blend with charming ease.

With the founding of an abbey in the 13th century, the village grew rich on the medieval wool industry and continued to prosper as an important coaching stop between Marlborough and Bristol until the mid-18th century when, as an estate-owned village, time seemed to stand still for nearly 100 years. Entirely owned and preserved by the National Trust since 1944, Lacock is amongst England's most beautiful villages and is, certainly, one of Wiltshire's most visited. If you're interested in architecture and plan to visit Lacock Abbey, allow the whole day and undertake the short stroll.

Fox Talbot and Lacock Abbey

Of all the outstanding buildings in the village Lacock Abbey, on the outskirts, is the most beautiful. It began as an Augustinian nunnery in 1232, but after the Reformation Sir William Sharrington used the remains to build a Tudor mansion, preserving the fine cloister court, sacristy and chapter house, and adding a romantic octagonal tower, a large courtyard and twisting chimney stacks.

The abbey passed to the Talbot family through marriage and they Gothicised the south elevation and added the famous oriel windows. Surrounded by peaceful water-meadows bordering the meandering River Avon, this was the setting for the experiments of William Henry Fox Talbot (1800–77), which in 1835 led to the creation of the world's first photographic negative. You can see some of Fox Talbot's work and equipment, alongside lively and interesting photographic exhibitions, in the beautifully restored 16th-century barn at the gates to the abbey.

Walk 38

Village Highlights

Architectural gems to note as you wander around Lacock's ancient streets include the timber-framed Sign of the Angel Inn, on Church Street, which retains its medieval layout, a 16th-century doorway and the passage through which horses would pass. Near by, Cruck House, with one its cruck beams exposed, is a rare example of this 14th-century building method. Further along, you will pass King John's Hunting Lodge, reputed to be even older than the abbey, and St Cyriac's Church which contains the grandiose Renaissance tomb of Sir William Sharrington. In West Street, the George Inn dates back to 1361 and features a huge open fire with a dogwheel which was connected to the spit on the fire and turned by a dog called a Turnspit. Next door to the pub take a quick look at the bus shelter; it was formerly the village smithy.

On the corner of East Street is the magnificent 14th-century tithe barn with fine curved timbers. This was once used to store the rents which were paid to the Abbey in kind, such as corn, hides and fleeces. The building later became the market hall as Lacock flourished into a thriving wool trading centre. Finally, don't miss the 18th-century domed lock-up next door. This is known as a 'blind house', since many of its overnight prisoners were drunks. You may recognise Lacock's medieval streets as the backdrop to several television costume dramas, notably Jane Austen's *Pride and Prejudice* (1995) and *Emma* (1996), and Daniel Defoe's rather bawdy *Moll Flanders* (1996).

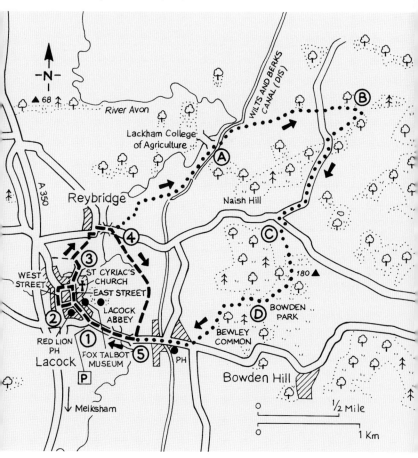

Walk 38 **Directions**

① From the car park entrance, cross the road and follow the gravel path into the village, passing the entrance to **Lacock Abbey** and the **Fox Talbot Museum**. Turn right into **East Street** opposite the Red Lion and walk down to **Church Street**. Turn left, pass the Sign of the Angel with its magnificent 16th-century doorway and bear left into **West Street** opposite the George Inn. Shortly, follow the road left into the **High Street**.

② Pass the National Trust shop and turn left to walk back down **East Street**. Turn right along the **Church Street** and bear left in front of **St Cyriac's Church** to reach an ancient packhorse bridge beside a ford across the **Bide Brook**. Follow the path beside the stream then up the lane beside cottages to the end of the road.

③ Go through the kissing gate on your right and follow the tarmac path across the field to a gate and pass the stone cottages at **Reybridge** to a lane. Turn right along the lane, then right again to cross the bridge over the **River Avon**.

④ Immediately cross the stile on your right and bear diagonally left to the far corner where you rejoin the riverbank to reach a stile. Walk beside the river for 300yds (274m) to a further stile and cross the field following the line of telegraph poles to a stile. Keep straight on to a stile beside a gate, then head towards the stone bridge over the **Avon**.

⑤ Climb the stile and turn right across the bridge. Join the raised pavement and follow it back into the village and car park.

Bowden Park

A longer loop takes in a disused canal and Bowden Park.
See map and information panel for Walk 38

•DISTANCE•	5½ miles (8.8km)
•MINIMUM TIME•	2hrs 30min
•ASCENT / GRADIENT•	426ft (130m) ▲▲ ▲
•LEVEL OF DIFFICULTY•	🚶 🚶 🚶

Walk 39 Directions
(Walk 38 option)

Cross the river bridge, at the end of the directions for Point ③, and take the stile on your left. Bear diagonally right across the field to a stile and cross the lane and stile opposite. Follow the path to two stiles and turn left around the field edge. Climb the stile on your left and turn right along the field edge, soon to follow the path through scrub to a stile. Proceed straight ahead with the remains of the **Wilts and Berks Canal** to your right.

The canal was opened in 1810 and linked Semington, on the Kennet and Avon Canal to Abingdon and the Thames in Oxfordshire, a distance of 51 miles (82km) with 42 locks. Coal from Somerset was its main cargo, and commercial traffic ceased in 1906.

Pass an old bridge, Point ④, climb a stile into woodland and turn immediately right along a narrow path to a stile. Turn left along the field edge, keep ahead across the next field to a stile and head uphill through scrub to a further stile. Proceed ahead to a gate and maintain direction across the next field to a gate. Join a track along the left-hand field edge, cross a farm drive and continue to a gate. Ascend the track to a gate and proceed uphill towards a house.

Before a gate turn right, Point ⑧, (field entrance left) across the top of the field below a house to reach double stiles. Bear half-right to a gate beside a cattle grid and ascend the farm drive through woodland, then continue uphill to a gate. Ignore the farm drive right and continue to the lane. Turn left, then cross the stile on the right before a house, Point ©. Keep to the left-hand edge of the field, cross a stile and bear diagonally left across the field to a stile in the corner. Cross the stile ahead into woodland and follow the path to a stile. Proceed ahead along the field edge to reach a stile on your right. Bear half-left across **Bowden Park**, keeping to the left of trees, and bear right down a track to a stile by a gate, Point ⑩.

Keep ahead downhill to a stile and turn left around the field edge to another stile and a gate near a house. Follow the path to the drive and follow it left. As tarmac gives way to gravel, bear off right across **Bewley Common** to the road junction. Turn right and keep to the road to cross the **River Avon** and return to **Lacock**.

Walk 40

Malmesbury and the Avon

An undemanding riverside stroll around a Saxon hilltop town.

•DISTANCE•	2 miles (3.2km)
•MINIMUM TIME•	1hr
•ASCENT / GRADIENT•	49ft (15m)
•LEVEL OF DIFFICULTY•	
•PATHS•	Field paths, town streets, 5 stiles
•LANDSCAPE•	River valley and urban area
•SUGGESTED MAP•	aqua3 OS Explorer 168 Stroud, Tetbury & Malmesbury
•START / FINISH•	Grid reference: ST 932875
•DOG FRIENDLINESS•	No problems on riverside pastures
•PARKING•	Yard car park (free)
•PUBLIC TOILETS•	Malmesbury town centre

Walk 40 Directions

A picturesque town of mellow
Cotswold stone, Malmesbury stands
between two branches of the River
Avon on the site of a Saxon fortified
hilltop town. Dominating the
surviving medieval street plan are
the impressive remains of a
Benedictine abbey, founded in the
7th century by St Aldhelm, its first
abbot. Malmesbury is one of the
oldest boroughs in England, the
original royal charter was granted
by King Alfred in AD 880 and
confirmed by King Athelstan
(reigned AD 925–939), when he
made Malmesbury his capital,
holding court just outside the town.
After the dissolution of the
monasteries in the 1540s, the abbey
was sold for £1,517 to a local wool
merchant, William Stumpe, who
presented the surviving nave to the

WHERE TO EAT AND DRINK ⓘ
Try the **Smoking Dog** for real ale and
decent food. Excellent coffee, afternoon
teas and light lunches are served in the
Old Bell Hotel.

---

townspeople for their parish
church. In the following centuries
several mills sprang up along the
local rivers and the town became an
important centre for the
manufacture of woollen cloth. It
later became renowned for
producing fine lace and silk.

From the car park, keep the river to
your right and walk towards the
abbey and **Abbey House**. At the
information board, bear left, then
right through a kissing gate into
Conygre Mead. Keep right along
the path and walk along the river
bank, noting the old railway tunnel
and Abbey House across the river.

Abbey House, a handsome Tudor
building, was built by William
Stumpe in the mid-16th century on
monastic foundations. It has an
5 acre (2ha) garden featuring one
of Britain's largest private
collections of roses.

At the road, go through a gate, turn
right across the bridge and descend
steps to reach a stile. At a fork of
paths, keep right across **Longmead**

Walk 40

to double stiles in the right-hand field corner. Take the left-hand path through the next field and walk along the river bank to a stile and footbridge. Cross the old sluice gate and continue to the lane beside **Wynyard Mill**. Turn right past the bowls club, following **St John Street** to **Lower High Street**.

St John Street has many ancient houses, notably a collection of almshouses from 1694 built on the site of St John the Baptist's Hospital. Incorporated in the gable wall is an early 13th-century arch. The Old Courthouse, through School Arch, is where the Old Corporation of Burgesses and Commoners have met since 1616. These are direct descendants of the men living in Malmesbury over 1,000 years ago to whom King Athelstan gave 500 acres (20ha) of common land (King's Heath) for their help in battle against the Danes, and this land is still passed down the generations.

Cross the road and go through the memorial gates and bear left along the walkway parallel to **St John's Bridge** to rejoin the road opposite **Avon Mills**. Turn right along the pavement and go through the gate on your right to follow the permissive path beside the **River Avon**. Cross a stile and keep to the path through gates and across various footbridges, soon to leave

the river, keeping beside the hedge to a gap in the field corner and a small stone bridge.

Cross the bridge, the path soon becomes paved, to reach a footbridge across the Avon. At a T-junction, turn left along **Burnivale**, then climb **Betty Geezers Steps** on your right to reach **Abbey Row**, with the Civic Trust Garden to your left. Cross the road and bear right in front of the **Old Bell Hotel** and enter the close to visit the abbey.

On the far side of Abbey Close is the 500-year-old Market Cross, an elaborate, octagonal building with a ribbed ceiling and intricate carvings, which was built for the market traders and buyers to stand in when it rained. The isolated steeple is the remnant of the 13th-century St Paul's Church, the parish church until 1541. This now serves as the bell tower for the abbey church. Among the more striking features of the abbey are the Norman porch, one of the finest in England, ablaze with exquisite carvings, the vaulted nave roof, the 14th-century stone screens in the north and south aisles, and the tomb of King Athelstan.

Return to the **Old Bell** and take the path immediately right for the **Cloister Garden**. Walk through the garden and turn left down steps, then right along **Mill Lane** back to the car park.

Sherston and Easton Grey's Cotswold Fringe

The infant Bristol Avon links attractive stone villages on this pastoral ramble on the south eastern fringes of the Cotswolds.

•DISTANCE•	6½ miles (10.4km)
•MINIMUM TIME•	3hrs
•ASCENT / GRADIENT•	131ft (40m) ▲▲▲
•LEVEL OF DIFFICULTY•	林林 林林 林林
•PATHS•	Field and parkland paths, tracks, metalled lanes, 11 stiles
•LANDSCAPE•	River valley and gently rolling farmland
•SUGGESTED MAP•	aqua3 OS Explorer 168 Stroud, Tetbury & Malmesbury
•START / FINISH•	Grid reference: ST 853858
•DOG FRIENDLINESS•	Dogs can be off lead along Fosse Way
•PARKING•	Sherston High Street; plenty of roadside parking
•PUBLIC TOILETS•	None on route

BACKGROUND TO THE WALK

The Bristol Avon rises in the foothills of the Cotswolds in the north west corner of Wiltshire and is little more than a wide and shallow stream as it flows through the gently rolling pastoral countryside west of Malmesbury. Despite its size, this peaceful river enhances all the charming little stone villages in this unspoilt and somewhat forgotten area of north Wiltshire, which is typically Cotswold in appearance and character. In fact, 18 villages between Colerne and Malmesbury are officially part of the Cotswold Area of Outstanding Natural Beauty. Of these, Sherston must rank among the most attractive, with its wide High Street, doubtless once used as a market, lined with some interesting 17th- and 18th-century buildings. Sherston was a borough by the 15th century and prospered as a result of the flourishing wool trade at the time. It still has the feel of a market town, with narrow back streets and alleys, and continues to be a thriving community despite becoming a dormitory village.

Legend of a Local Hero

It has been suggested that Sherston is Sceorstan, as chronicled by Henry of Huntingdon, where in 1016 Edmund Ironside won a battle against the Danes who were led by King Canute. The early legend of John Rattlebone, a local yeoman promised land by Ironside in return for service against the Danes is deep rooted. Sadly, this brave knight was terribly wounded in battle and although he staunched his bleeding with a stone tile and continued fighting, he reputedly died as Canute's army withdrew. Other traditions say Rattlebone survived to claim his reward. In the 17th century, the antiquary John Aubrey recorded the following local rhyme: 'Fight well, Rattlebone, Thou shalt have Sherston, What shall I with Sherston do, Without I have all belongs thereto? Thou shalt have Wych and Wellesley, Easton Town and Pinkeney'.

Later traditions tell us that the small stone effigy on the south side of the porch outside the parish church is that of Rattlebone, and that an ancient timber chest in the church,

Walk 41

marked with the initials R B, is supposed to be where Rattlebone kept his armour. Whatever the truth is, the Rattlebone Inn opposite the church keeps his name alive, its sign showing Rattlebone in action.

Easton Grey – Pure Cotswold Charm

Peaceful parkland and riverside paths lead you downstream to picturesque Easton Grey. Set around a 16th-century stone bridge and climbing a short, curving street is an intimate huddle of ancient stone houses, with mullioned windows, steep, lichen-covered roofs and colourful, flower-filled gardens that touch the river bank. Set back on a rise above the river is Easton Grey House, a handsome 18th-century manor house with a classical façade and portico, surrounded by elegant gardens and lovely valley views. It was the summer retreat of Herbert Asquith, 1st Earl of Oxford, when he was Prime Minister between 1908 and 1916.

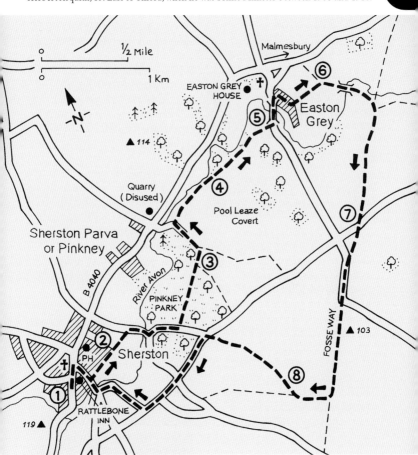

Walk 41 Directions

① On Sherton's High Street, walk towards the village stores, pass the **Rattlebone Inn** and turn right into

Noble Street. Pass Grove Road and take the footpath left up a flight of steps. Cross a cul-de-sac and follow the metalled footpath to a gate. Continue to the rear of houses to a further gate.

Walk 41

② Bear diagonally right across a field to a gate and lane. Turn right, cross the river and turn left, signed '**Foxley**'. At the end of woodland on your left, take the footpath left through a gate. Follow the track across **Pinkney Park** to a gate.

③ Keep ahead, bearing left beside the wall to a gate. Follow the track ahead towards farm buildings and where the drive curves left, turn right into the farmyard. Keep right to join a concrete path to a stile. Turn left around the field edge to a stile and keep to the left-hand field edge to a stile in the corner.

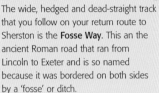

WHAT TO LOOK FOR

The wide, hedged and dead-straight track that you follow on your return route to Sherston is the **Fosse Way**. This an the ancient Roman road that ran from Lincoln to Exeter and is so named because it was bordered on both sides by a 'fosse' or ditch.

WHERE TO EAT AND DRINK

Rest weary limbs and refuel at the **Rattlebone Inn** in Sherston. A lively inn with a great atmosphere, the rambling bars are the setting for hearty lunchtime snacks and imaginative evening meals with decent wine and Youngs ales. Alternatively, try the **Carpenters Arms** which is noted for fresh fish.

④ Bear half-right across the field to follow the path along the field edge above the River Avon to a stile. Cross a further stile and walk beside the fence, with **Easton Grey House** left, and head downhill to a gate and lane.

⑤ Turn left into **Easton Grey**. Cross the river bridge, turn right uphill to take the footpath ahead on reaching entrance gates on your right. Cross a gravelled area, go through a gate and keep ahead to a

stile. Maintain direction across the next field and gently descend to follow a track into the next field.

⑥ Turn right along the field edge and bear off right downhill through scrub to a footbridge. Keep ahead beside a ruin to a gate. Cross a stile and continue to a further stile and gate. Follow the track downhill to a stile and turn right along a track (**Fosse Way**). Continue for ½ mile (800m) to a road.

⑦ Cross straight over and keep to the byway to another road. Bear left and keep ahead where the lane veers sharp left. Follow this rutted track for ½ mile (800m), then cross the arrowed stile on your right. Head straight across the field to a gate and bear diagonally right across a large paddock to a stile.

⑧ Join a track, cross a racehorse gallop and go through the left-hand gate ahead. Walk through scrub to another gate and keep to the track ahead to a road. Turn left and continue to a crossroads. Proceed straight on to the next junction and keep ahead, following the lane all the way back into **Sherston**.

WHILE YOU'RE THERE

Nearby **Luckington Court Gardens**, TV film location for Jane Austen's *Pride and Prejudice* (1995), has a 3 acre (1.2ha) formal garden and a walled flower garden. Head north just across the border into Gloucestershire to visit **Westonbirt Arboretum**, one of the finest and most important collections of trees and shrubs in the country. Visit in spring for the impressive displays of rhododendrons, azaleas, magnolias and wild flowers, and later in the year for the magnificent autumn colours.

Box **107**

Brunel's Great Tunnel Through Box Hill

A hilly walk around Box Hill, famous for its stone and Brunel's greatest engineering achievement.

•DISTANCE•	3¼ miles (5.3km)
•MINIMUM TIME•	1hr 45min
•ASCENT / GRADIENT•	508ft (155m) ▲▲▲
•LEVEL OF DIFFICULTY•	🚶🚶 🚶🚶 🚶
•PATHS•	Field and woodland paths, bridle paths, metalled lanes, 15 stiles
•LANDSCAPE•	River valley and wooded hillsides
•SUGGESTED MAP•	aqua3 OS Explorer 156 Chippenham & Bradford-on-Avon
•START / FINISH•	Grid reference: ST 823686
•DOG FRIENDLINESS•	Can be off lead on Box Hill Common and in woodland
•PARKING•	Village car park near Selwyn Hall
•PUBLIC TOILETS•	Opposite Queens Head in Box

BACKGROUND TO THE WALK

Box is a large straggling village that sits astride the busy A4 in hilly country halfway between Bath and Chippenham. Although stone has been quarried here since the 9th century, Box really found fame during the 18th-century when the local stone was used for Bath's magnificent buildings. The construction of Box Tunnel also uncovered immense deposits of good stone and by 1900 Box stone quarries were among the most productive in the world, employing over 700 men. Little trace can be seen above ground today, except for some fine stone-built houses in the village and a few reminders of the industry on Box Hill.

Appointed Engineer

In 1833, the newly created Great Western Railway appointed Isambard Kingdom Brunel (1806–59) as engineer. His task was to build a railway covering the 118 miles (190km) from London to Bristol. The problems and projects he encountered on the way would help to make him the most famous engineer of the Victorian age. After a relatively straightforward and level start through the Home Counties, which earned the nickname 'Brunel's Billiard Table', he came to the hilly Cotswolds. (Incidentally, the Provost of Eton thought the line would be injurious to the discipline of the school and the morals of the pupils.)

Brunel's Famous Tunnel

The solution at Box would be a tunnel, and at nearly 2 miles (3.2km) long and with a gradient of 1:100 it would be the longest and steepest in the world at the time. It would also be very wide. Already controversial, Brunel ignored the gauge of other companies, preferring the 7ft (2.1m) used by tramways and roads (and, it was believed, Roman chariots). He also made the tunnel dead straight, and, never one to 'hide his light', the alignment was calculated so the dawn sun would shine through on his birthday on 9th April. Unfortunately he did not allow for atmospheric refraction and was two days out!

Passage to Narnia?

All was on a grand scale: a ton of gunpowder and candles was used every week, 3 million bricks were fired to line the soft Cotswold limestone and 100 navvies lost their lives working on the tunnel. After 2½ years the way was open, and although Brunel would ultimately lose the battle of the gauges, his magnificent line meant that Bristol was then a mere two hours from the capital. Although artificial, like many large dark holes, the tunnel has collected its fair share of mystery with tales of noises, people under the hill and trains entering the tunnel, never to re-emerge. But as is often the case, the explanations are rather more mundane. To test excavation conditions, Brunel dug a small trial section alongside what is now the eastern entrance and the military commandeered this section during World War Two as a safe and fairly secret store for ammunition, records and top brass. Sadly it is not a passage to Narnia!

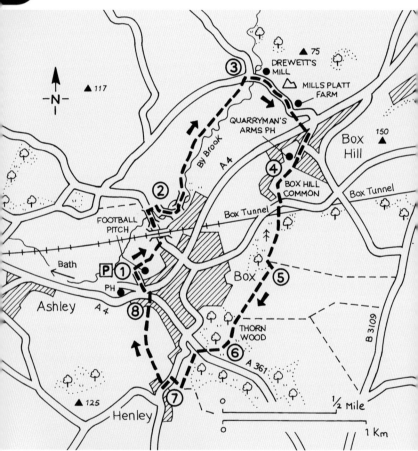

Walk 42 Directions

① Facing the **recreation ground**, walk to the left-hand side of the football pitch to join a track in the corner close to the railway line. When you reach the lane, turn left, pass beneath the railway, cross a bridge and take the arrowed footpath, to the right, before the second bridge.

Box **109**

WHILE YOU'RE THERE ⓘ
Visit **Haselbury Manor** at Wadswick (east off B3109) for its recently restored, richly varied landscaped gardens, with stone and yew circles, a rockery, formal gardens, rose gardens and laburnum walk. Visit the **heritage centre** in nearby Corsham to learn more about the Bath stone quarrying industry in the area.

② Walk beside the river, cross a footbridge and turn right. Cross a further footbridge and continue to a stile. Walk through water-meadows close to the river, go through a squeeze stile and maintain direction. Shortly, bear left to a squeeze stile in the field corner. Follow the right-hand field edge to a stile and lane.

③ Turn right, then right again at the junction. Cross the river, pass **Drewett's Mill** and steeply ascend the lane. Just past **Mills Platt Farm**, take the arrowed footpath ahead across a stile. Continue steeply uphill to a stile and cross the A4. Ascend steps to a lane and proceed straight on up **Barnetts Hill**. Keep right at the fork, then right again and pass the **Quarryman's Arms**.

④ Keep left at the fork and continue beside **Box Hill Common** to a junction. Take the path straight ahead into woodland. Almost

immediately, fork left and follow the path close to the woodland edge. As it curves right into the beech wood, bear left and follow the path through the gap in the wall and then immediately right at the junction of paths.

⑤ Follow the bridle path to a fork. Keep left, then turn right at the T-junction and take the path left to a stile. Cross a further stile and descend into **Thorn Wood**, following the stepped path to a stile at the bottom.

⑥ Continue through scrub to a stile and turn right beside the fence to a wall stile. Bear right to a further stile, then bear left uphill to a stile and the **A361**. Cross over and follow the drive ahead. Where it curves left by stables, keep ahead along the arrowed path to a house. Bear right up the garden steps to the drive and continue uphill to a T-junction.

⑦ Turn left, then on entering **Henley**, take the path right, across a stile. Follow the field edge to a stile and descend to an allotment and stile. Continue to a stile and gate.

⑧ Follow the drive ahead, bear left at the garage and take the metalled path right, into **Box**. Cross the main road and continue to the **A4**. Turn right, then left down the access road back to **Selwyn Hall**.

WHAT TO LOOK FOR ⓘ
Explore Box and locate the **Blind House** on the main street, one of a dozen in Wiltshire for disturbers of the peace. Look for **Coleridge House**, named after the poet who often broke his journey here on his way to Nether Stowey. Also look for the former **Candle Factory** on the Rudloe road that once produced the candles used during the building of Box Tunnel, and head east along the A4 for the best view of the **tunnel's entrance**.

WHERE TO EAT AND DRINK ⓘ
In Box, you will find both the **Queen's Head** and **Bayly's** offer good food and ale in convivial surroundings. Time your walk for opening time at the **Quarryman's Arms** on Box Hill. Enjoy the views across Box from the dining room with a pint of locally-brewed ale, just like the local stone miners once did.

Stourhead's Paradise

A gentle walk through the Stourhead Estate.

•**DISTANCE**•	3 miles (4.8km)
•**MINIMUM TIME**•	1hr 30min
•**ASCENT / GRADIENT**•	262ft (80m) ▲▲▲
•**LEVEL OF DIFFICULTY**•	𝟰 𝟰 𝟰
•**PATHS**•	Parkland and woodland paths and tracks, 2 stiles
•**LANDSCAPE**•	Woodland and parkland
•**SUGGESTED MAP**•	aqua3 OS Explorers 142 Shepton Mallet; 143 Warminster & Trowbridge
•**START / FINISH**•	Grid reference: ST 779340 (on Explorer 142)
•**DOG FRIENDLINESS**•	Under control through Stourhead Estate; off lead on White Sheet Hill. No dogs in Stourhead Gardens March–October
•**PARKING**•	Free National Trust car park at Stourton
•**PUBLIC TOILETS**•	Stourhead Visitor Centre and Spread Eagle courtyard

BACKGROUND TO THE WALK

Although without the immediate charm of similar estate villages like Lacock and Castle Combe, Stourton enjoys an idyllic setting in a valley on the edge of the Stourhead Estate. Beautifully preserved, consisting of a pleasing group of 18th-century cottages, an inn, St Peter's Church and a graceful medieval cross, its unique atmosphere is attributable to the glorious views across a lake and one of Europe's finest landscaped parkland gardens.

Wealthy banker Henry Hoare acquired Stourhead in 1717. He promptly pulled down medieval Stourton House, and commissioned Colen Campbell, the foremost architect and designer of the day, to build a new Palladian style house. Extended in the 1780s by Sir Richard Colt Hoare, the magnificent interior includes an outstanding Regency library, a significant collection of Chippendale furniture and fine paintings in the elegant gallery.

A Taste of Paradise

But Stourhead is more famous for its gardens, designed by Henry Hoare II and laid out between 1741 and 1745. Now in the care of the National Trust, they are an outstanding example of the English landscape style. Inspired by the landscapes he had seen in Italy and by the artists Claude Lorraine and Nicholas Poussin, Hoare set out to create a poetic landscape at Stourhead. Having dammed the River Stour and diverted the medieval fish ponds to create a large lake, he began his three-dimensional 'painting', planting beechwoods to clothe the hills and frame new lakes. Classical temples, including the Pantheon and the Temple of Apollo, were skillfully located around the central lake at the end of a series of vistas, which change as you stroll around the estate. You will find the gardens a memorable place to visit at any time, but walk this way in spring for the spectacular display of rhododendrons and azaleas, and in late October for the beautiful autumnal colours.

This walk explores some of the tranquil tracks and paths that criss-cross the surrounding farmland and woodland. Along the way, at Park Hill, you will cross a large bank, formerly the boundary to the original deer park created in 1448 by John Stourton, and pass an Iron-Age hill fort covering 6 acres (2.4ha).

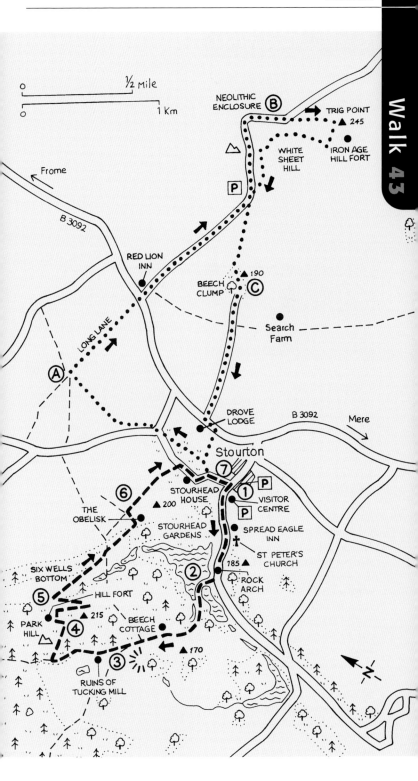

NEOLITHIC ENCLOSURE Ⓑ
TRIG POINT ▲ 245
WHITE SHEET HILL
IRON AGE HILL FORT

Frome

B 3092

Ⓟ

RED LION INN

BEECH CLUMP ▲ 190 Ⓒ

Search Farm

Ⓐ

LONG LANE

DROVE LODGE

B 3092 Mere

Stourton

⑦

Ⓟ

STOURHEAD HOUSE
① VISITOR CENTRE

Ⓟ

⑥
THE OBELISK

▲ 200

STOURHEAD GARDENS
② SPREAD EAGLE INN

ST PETER'S CHURCH
▲ 185

SIX WELLS BOTTOM
⑤ HILL FORT

ROCK ARCH

④ ▲ 215
PARK HILL

BEECH COTTAGE
③ ▲ 170

RUINS OF TUCKING MILL

½ Mile
1 Km

Walk **43**

Walk 43 **Directions**

① Leave the car park via the exit and turn left down the lane into **Stourton** village passing the Spread Eagle Inn, St Peter's Church and the entrance to Stourhead Gardens. (Note: National Trust members or those paying to visit the Gardens and Stourhead House should access the village via the visitor centre.) Continue along the lane, pass beneath the **Rock Arch** and turn immediately right along a track.

WHERE TO EAT AND DRINK
Adjacent to the car park is the National Trust's restaurant serving teas, coffees and light lunches. Alternatively, enjoy a pint and a ploughman's at the **Spread Eagle** in the village or stop at the **Red Lion** below White Sheet Hill.

---

② Pass beside the lake, cross a cattle grid and follow the track to **Beech Cottage**. Keep left along the track, to a stile beside a gate and ignore the Stour Valley Way signposted to the right. At a fork, bear right through the gate, signed 'Alfred's Tower'.

③ Proceed ahead on the grassy track along the top of the field to a further gate and stile, noting the ruins of **Tucking Mill and Cottages** on your left. Walk through the woodland and take the first track right (by a silver National Trust sign) into coniferous woodland. Ascend steeply to reach **Broad Ride**, a wide grassy swathe through the woodland.

④ Turn left to a gate and the Iron-Age hill fort at **Park Hill**. Do not cross the stile, but bear right along the narrow path beside the fence to reach a track. Turn right and

shortly turn sharp left downhill through the woodland to a stile and **Six Wells Bottom**.

⑤ Turn right and bear diagonally left across the valley bottom, keeping left of the lake, heading uphill to a gate on the edge of woodland. Continue up the track to a gate and turn immediately left up the bank to pass the **Obelisk**, with **Stourhead House** clearly visible now to your right.

⑥ On reaching the track, turn right towards **Stourhead House**. At a junction of tracks, turn right through a gate and pass in front of the house. Walk down the drive then, where it curves right, take the waymarked path left through a gate to start of Walk 44.

WHILE YOU'RE THERE
Don't miss climbing **King Alfred's Tower** on the edge of the Stourhead Estate. This intriguing red brick folly, built in 1772, stands 160ft (48m) high and affords magnificent views across Somerset, Dorset and Wiltshire.

---

⑦ To finish this short loop (Walk 43), pass underneath the gate house and turn left up the lane back to the car park. National Trust members and visitors that have paid to enter the Stourhead gardens and house can bear right just before the gatehouse and walk through the walled garden and across a bridge to return to the car park via the **visitor centre**.

WHAT TO LOOK FOR
In Beech Clump below White Sheet Hill, look out for the **memorial** dedicated to the airmen who lost lost their lives in Dakota TS436 No 107OTU Leicester East, which crashed here after taking off from RAF Zeals on 19th February 1945.

White Sheet Hill

A longer loop to a neolithic camp and a hill fort on White Sheet Hill.
See map and information panel for Walk 43

•DISTANCE•	5 miles (8km)
•MINIMUM TIME•	4hrs
•ASCENT / GRADIENT•	344ft (105m) ▲▲▲
•LEVEL OF DIFFICULTY•	🚶 🚶 🚶

Walk 44 Directions (Walk 43 option)

From the gate, Point ⑦, beside the main drive follow the path straight across the parkland in front of **Stourhead House**. Merge with a track and keep ahead through two gates to a lane. Cross the stile opposite and bear half-left across a field to a stile located between telegraph poles. Climb a further stile and continue ahead to the left of fencing, following the grass track to a stile in the corner, Point Ⓐ. Drop down steps and turn right along the sunken bridleway (**Long Lane**) to reach the B3092, opposite the **Red Lion Inn**. Cross straight over and follow the lane towards White Sheet Hill. Pass a parking area and continue steeply uphill, following the track sharp right to pass through the neolithic enclosure on **White Sheet Hill**.

White Sheet Hill is rich in prehistoric monuments, including a rare causewayed enclosure, one of the earliest types of British earthworks. This neolithic camp consists of a ring of short banks and ditches built about 5,500 years ago. Evidence suggests prehistoric local farmers met here for markets, fairs or religious ceremonies, and it was probably not built for defence purposes or to enclose village sites, unlike the high ramparts and deep ditches of the adjacent Iron-Age hill fort which dates from 500 BC.

Continue along the track and cross the stile on your right by the information board, Point Ⓑ. Turn left alongside the fence to reach the Iron-Age fort. At the trig point, cut across the centre of the fort and bear right along the path on top of the rampart and continue along the scarp edge. Admire the views west across Stourhead Estate to King Alfred's Tower on the skyline and south east across the Blackmore Vale to the Dorset Downs beyond.

Cross a stile at the top of the old quarry and bear left alongside the fence, heading downhill to a stile. Keep left through the car park and follow the track to a gate. Proceed ahead, pass through **Beech Clump**, Point Ⓒ, and continue on the wide track, crossing two stiles, to reach a gate and the **B3092** opposite **Drove Lodge**. Turn left for 50yds (46m), then take the footpath right through trees to a stile. Walk straight across parkland towards **Stourhead House** and join your outward route back to the main drive and Walk 43 at Point ⑦.

Westbury White Horse

An exhilarating downland walk to a famous white horse.

•DISTANCE•	4 miles (6.4km)
•MINIMUM TIME•	2hrs 30min
•ASCENT / GRADIENT•	557ft (170m) ▲▲▲
•LEVEL OF DIFFICULTY•	🏃🏃 🏃🏃 🏃🏃
•PATHS•	Field paths and downland tracks, 1 stile
•LANDSCAPE•	Downland
•SUGGESTED MAP•	aqua3 OS Explorer 143 Warminster & Trowbridge
•START / FINISH•	Grid reference: ST 914523
•DOG FRIENDLINESS•	Let dogs off lead on top of Westbury Hill
•PARKING•	Jubilee Hall in Tynings Lane, Bratton, just off B3098
•PUBLIC TOILETS•	None on route

Walk 45 Directions

The most notable feature of Bratton, a large modern village in the shadow of a huge downland escarpment, is the Church of St James the Great, arguably one of the most charming churches in the county. Reached by a series of steep steps, and nestling at the base of the chalk downland, it dates from the 13th century and is worth the climb to view the traces of Norman architecture and the wildly grinning gargoyles.

Turn right out of the car park to the **B3098**. Turn left, then almost immediately left again up **Butts Lane**. Fork right into **Upper Garston Lane** by the **Oratory of St Giles** then, just before the lane dips, take the path left, waymarked

WHERE TO EAT AND DRINK ⓘ
Refresh yourselves after this taxing downland walk at the **Duke** in Bratton, noted for its generous home-cooked food, including excellent Sunday roasts, and Moles ales.

to the church. Descend steps, cross a brook, then climb steps to the church gates. Take the narrow path right and ascend through trees. Ignore the stile on your left and climb the stile ahead into pasture at the base of downland.

Follow the permissive path half-right up the field, passing through a belt of trees, then climb diagonally up the scarp slope to the fence at the top. Keep right alongside the fence, go through a gate, then turn right through a metal gate to follow a sunken track around the top of **Combe Bottom**. At the lane, turn left uphill and soon take the track, right, on to the outer rampart of **Bratton Camp**. Bear right to follow the outer rampart path to reach the **Westbury White Horse** hill figure.

Westbury Hill rises to the commanding height of 750ft (229m) above sea level and forms the dramatic western edge of Salisbury Plain. The views are tremendous, with the scarp slope dropping into the Vale of Pewsey, and on the horizon, on a clear day,

WHAT TO LOOK FOR

Make sure you pause at the viewpoint pillar on **Westbury Hill**, especially on a clear day, as you will be surprised just how far reaching the view is. Walk this way in spring and early summer to see the grassy downland summit and slopes alive with chalk loving plants, such as bird's foot trefoil, and butterflies like the chalkhill blue.

you can see across Somerset to the Mendips and the Cotswolds. Dominating the hilltop is Bratton Castle, an Iron-Age hill fort covering 25 acres (10ha) of the plateau and defended by double banks and ditches rising to 35ft (11m). The long barrow inside the fort is a burial mound probably built before 3000 BC.

Cut into the side of the hill, just below the castle ramparts, is Wiltshire's oldest and best known white horse measuring 180ft (55m) long and 108ft (33m) high. This graceful hill figure is believed to have replaced a much earlier and cruder creature which local tradition states was cut in celebration of King Alfred's victory over the Danes at the Battle of Ethundun in AD 878. The present, well-proportioned animal, which is featured on the bottles of a brand of whisky of the same name, was cut

WHILE YOU'RE THERE

Make the short trip east along the B3098 to Edington to see the impressive, cathedral-like **Church of St Mary, St Katherine and All Saints**. It is an architectural treasure, built in 1351 as part of a priory founded by William of Edington, Bishop of Winchester, for Augustinian monks. There is much to marvel at including a rare wooden screen of 1500 and one of the oldest clocks in England, so pick up a church guide.

by a Mr Gee, steward to Lord Abingdon, in 1778, apparently because he objected to the primitive dog-like creature which had previously existed on Westbury Hill. The White Horse was remodelled in 1853 and restored 20 years later, with its most recent makeover in concrete, courtesy of Westbury Cement Works. This is the unmistakable industrial complex you can see in the valley below.

Shortly, leave the rampart and pass through a gate on to **Westbury Hill**. Keep to the path, passing benches and a viewpoint pillar, and soon reach a track. Turn left, pass the car park entrance and turn right at the T-junction. Pass **White Horse Farm** and turn left along the track to join the **Imber Range Perimeter Path**.

This is a 30 mile (48km) trail circumnavigating the Army's largest live firing range in the south of England. For over 50 years an area of Salisbury Plain 10 miles (16.1km) long and 5 miles (8km) wide has been occupied by the Army and public access has been very limited. Your view south is across the great central plateau, a wild and lonely landscape, full of mystery and a sense of space.

Keep to the track for ¾ mile (1.2km) to a barn and take the bridle path left through a gate. Follow the track past a copse into a field and keep to the left-hand edge to a gate. Bear right steeply down a sunken track towards **Bratton**. Go through a gate and descend through trees and keep ahead on reaching a metalled lane. Turn left at the T-junction, then bear left up a cobbled path (**The Ball**) between cottages. At the road, keep left back to the hall and car park.

Corsham – a Wealthy Weaving Town

Explore this unexpected architectural treasure of a town and the adjacent Corsham Park.

•DISTANCE•	4 miles (6.4km)
•MINIMUM TIME•	2hrs
•ASCENT / GRADIENT•	114ft (35m)
•LEVEL OF DIFFICULTY•	
•PATHS•	Field paths and country lanes, 10 stiles
•LANDSCAPE•	Town streets, gently undulating parkland, farmland
•SUGGESTED MAP•	aqua3 OS Explorer 156 Chippenham & Bradford on Avon
•START / FINISH•	Grid reference: ST 871704
•DOG FRIENDLINESS•	Can be off lead in Corsham Park
•PARKING•	Long stay car park in Newlands Lane
•PUBLIC TOILETS•	Short stay car park by shopping precinct

BACKGROUND TO THE WALK

Warm, cream-coloured Bath stone characterises this handsome little market town situated on the southern edge of the Cotswolds. An air of prosperity pervades the streets where the 15th-century Flemish gabled cottages and baroque-pedimented 17th-century Hungerford Almshouses mix with larger Georgian residences. Architectural historian Nikolaus Pevsner wrote: 'Corsham has no match in Wiltshire for the wealth of good houses'. The town owes its inheritance to the once thriving industries of cloth manufacture and stone quarrying during the 17th and 18th centuries.

Architectural Delights

Spend some time exploring the heart of the town before setting off across Corsham Park, as many of the fine stone buildings along the High Street, Church Street and Priory Street have been well preserved. Begin your town stroll at the Heritage Centre in the High Street (No 31), where interactive displays and hands-on exhibits present the stories of the weaving industry and quarrying of the golden Bath stone, which was used to create the architectural legacy of the town. In fact, No 31 once belonged to a prosperous 18th-century clothier, and No 70 (now an electrical shop) was the workhouse providing labour for the cloth industry. The Town Hall was formerly the market hall with one storey and open arches before being converted in 1882. North of the post office you will see the unspoilt line of 17th-century weavers' cottages. Known as the Flemish Buildings, this was the centre of the cloth industry where the Flemish weavers settled following religious persecution in their homeland. In Church Street, note the gabled cottages of the 18th-century weavers, with their ornate porches and a door on the first floor for taking in the raw wool.

Corsham Court – the Methuen Family Home

The finest of the houses is Corsham Court, a splendid Elizabethan mansion built in 1582 on the site of a medieval royal manor. It was bought in 1745 by Paul Methuen, a wealthy clothier and ancestor of the present owner, to house the family's collection of 16th- and 17th-century Italian and Flemish Master paintings and statuary. The house and park you see today are principally the work of 'Capability' Brown, John Nash and Thomas Bellamy. Brown built the gabled wings that house the state rooms and magnificent 72ft (22m) long picture gallery and laid out the park, including the avenues, Gothic bath house and the 13-acre (5ha) lake. Round off your walk with a tour of the house. You will see the outstanding collection of over 140 paintings, including pictures by Rubens, Turner, Reynolds and Van Dyck, fine statuary and bronzes, and the famous collection of English furniture, notably pieces by Robert Adam and Thomas Chippendale. You may recognise the house as the backdrop for the film *The Remains of the Day* (1993) starring Anthony Hopkins.

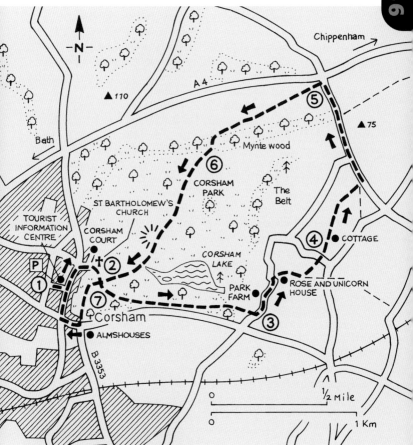

Walk 46 Directions

① Turn left out of the car park, then left again along **Post Office Lane** to reach the **High Street**. Turn left, pass the tourist information centre and turn right into **Church Street**. Pass the impressive entrance to Corsham Court and enter **St Bartholomew's churchyard**.

② Follow the path left to a gate and walk ahead to join the main path across **Corsham Park**. Turn left and walk along the south side of the

Walk 46

park, passing **Corsham Lake**, to reach a stile and gate. Keep straight on along a fenced path beside a track to a kissing gate and proceed across a field to a stile and lane.

③ Turn left, pass **Park Farm**, a splendid stone farmhouse on your left, and shortly take the waymarked footpath right along a drive to pass **Rose and Unicorn House**. Cross a stile and follow the right-hand field edge to a stile, then bear half-left to a stone stile in the field corner. Ignore the path arrowed right and head straight across the field to a further stile and lane.

④ Take the footpath opposite, bearing half-left to a stone stile to the left of a cottage. Maintain direction and pass through a field entrance to follow the path along the left-hand side of a field to a stile in the corner. Turn left along the road for ½ mile (800m) to the **A4**.

⑤ Go through the gate in the wall on your left and follow the worn path right, across the centre of

parkland pasture to a metal kissing gate. Proceed ahead to reach a kissing gate on the edge of woodland. Follow the wide path to a further gate and bear half-right to a stile.

⑥ Keep ahead on a worn path across the field and along the field edge to a gate. Continue to a further gate with fine views right to **Corsham Court**. Follow the path right along the field edge, then where it curves right, bear left to join the path beside the churchyard wall to a stile.

⑦ Turn left down the avenue of trees to a gate and the town centre, noting the stone almshouses on your left. Turn right along **Pickwick Road** and then right again along the pedestrianised **High Street**. Turn left back along **Post Office Lane** to the car park.

The Longleat Estate

Combine glorious woodland and parkland walking, through the Longleat Estate, with a visit to an opulent Elizabethan mansion.

•DISTANCE•	5¼ miles (8.4km)
•MINIMUM TIME•	2hrs 30min (longer if visiting Longleat attractions)
•ASCENT / GRADIENT•	508ft (155m) ▲ ▲ ▲
•LEVEL OF DIFFICULTY•	🚶 🚶 🚶
•PATHS•	Field, woodland and parkland paths, roads, 4 stiles
•LANDSCAPE•	Wooded hillside, village streets, parkland
•SUGGESTED MAP•	aqua3 OS Explorer 143 Warminster & Trowbridge
•START / FINISH•	Grid reference: ST 827422
•DOG FRIENDLINESS•	On leads through grounds
•PARKING•	Heaven's Gate car park, Longleat Estate
•PUBLIC TOILETS•	Longleat attractions complex

BACKGROUND TO THE WALK

Your first view of Longleat is an unforgettable one. As you stroll down the azalea and rhododendron lined path to Heaven's Gate, nothing prepares you for the superb panorama that stretches to the distant Mendip Hills. Central to this composition is Longleat House, an exquisite Elizabethan stone manor in a glorious, wooded, lakeside setting that looks more like a fairy-tale palace from a distance.

Longleat was the first stately home in Britain to open its doors to the public as a commercial proposition, first doing so in 1949, a trend which many would follow. Lions made Longleat famous in 1966 and since then the Marquess of Bath's home has amassed an ever-expanding roll-call of family attractions to keep it viable, including a safari park, hedged mazes, safari boats, a Dr Who exhibition and a Postman Pat village. Thankfully, there are also thousands of acres of landscaped parkland and estate woodland to explore, so you can escape the summer crowds and enjoy the wonderful setting.

Majestic Mansion

The hub of all this tourist activity is the Elizabethan mansion. Architect and builder Sir John Thynne, an ancestor of the Marquess of Bath, completed the house in 1580 on a site chosen for its beauty. The house was revolutionary in its design as it showed no thought for defence, its great bayed walls of stone and mullioned glass windows setting a new trend for Elizabethan architecture.

The splendid exterior is more than matched by the inside. Longleat contains a mixture of furnishings and artefacts reflecting the tastes and interests of the Thynne family throughout the centuries to the flamboyant 7th Marquess of Bath who owns Longleat today. Notable artefacts include a 33ft (10m) long 16th-century oak shuffle-board, a 17th-century gilt steeplechase cup and a library table commissioned from John Makepeace. Rich 17th-century Flemish tapestries, Genoese velvet and ancient Spanish leather clothe the walls, while painted ceilings, inspired by Italian palace interiors, including the Ducal Palace in Venice, and marble fireplaces ornament the state rooms. A tour will also reveal a fine collection of paintings, from 16th-century portraits and 18th-century Dutch paintings to early Italian pictures and notable hunting scenes. The fully restored Victorian kitchens give an interesting picture of life below stairs.

'Artist' Lord Bath

The colourful current Lord Bath began painting in the early 1960s and covered his private rooms in the West Wing with an amazing cycle of paintings. Expressing 'key hole glimpses of his psyche' are vast murals with satirical and erotic love scenes, while on the staircase hang the portraits of his numerous 'wifelets', or mistresses, in chronological order. Although a bearded Bohemian man in his sixties, he is also a sound businessman who has turned Longleat into a thriving, multi-million pound tourist attraction.

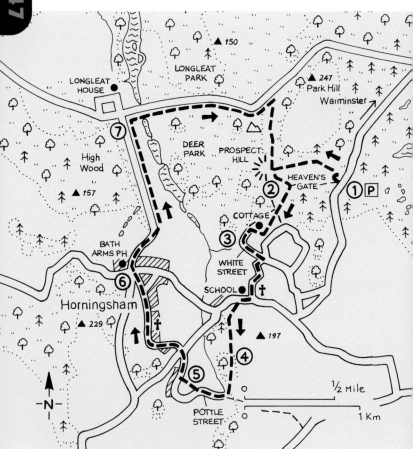

Walk 47 Directions

① Cross the road and follow the path into the trees. Disregard the straight track left, bear right and then left along a wide worn path through mixed woodland to double

gates and reach the viewpoint at **Heaven's Gate**.

② Facing Longleat, go through the gate in the left-hand corner. In 100yds (91m) at a crossing of paths, turn right, then keep right at a fork and head downhill through

Walk 47

woodland to a metalled drive by a thatched cottage. Turn right, keep ahead where the drive bears left, and shortly follow the path left, heading downhill close to the woodland edge to pass between a garage and cottage to a lane.

③ Turn left along **White Street** to a crossroads and turn right downhill. Ascend past the church to a T-junction and turn right. Turn left opposite the school, following the bridle path up a track and between sheds to a gate. Bear left with the grassy track, pass through two gates and bear slightly right to a stile on the edge of woodland.

④ Follow the path through the copse and soon bear off right diagonally downhill to a stile and gate. Turn left along the field edge to reach a track. Turn right, go through a gate beside a thatched cottage and follow the metalled lane (**Pottle Street**). In 200yds (183m), cross the stile on your right and cross the field to a stile and rejoin the lane.

⑤ Turn right and follow this quiet lane to a crossroads. Proceed straight across and follow the road through **Horningsham** village, passing the thatched chapel, to the crossroads opposite the **Bath Arms**.

⑥ Go straight across the crossroads, walk down the estate drive and pass through the gatehouse arch into **Longleat Park**. With the magnificent house ahead of you, walk beside the metalled drive with the lakes and weirs to your right. At a T-junction in front of the house, keep ahead to visit the house and follow the path left to reach the other tourist attractions.

⑦ For the main route, turn right and walk beside the drive, heading uphill through the **Deer Park**. Begin to climb steeply, then take the metalled drive right beyond a white barrier. With beautiful views across the parkland, gently ascend **Prospect Hill** and reach **Heaven's Gate** viewpoint. Retrace your steps back to the car park.

Bradford-on-Avon

Combine a visit to this enchanting riverside town with a canal-side stroll.

•DISTANCE•	3½ miles (5.7km)
•MINIMUM TIME•	1hr 45min
•ASCENT / GRADIENT•	164ft (50m) ▲ ▲ ▲
•LEVEL OF DIFFICULTY•	🚶 🚶 🚶
•PATHS•	Tow path, field and woodland paths, metalled lanes
•LANDSCAPE•	Canal, river valley, wooded hillsides, town streets
•SUGGESTED MAP•	aqua3 OS Explorers 142 Shepton Mallet;156 Chippenham & Bradford-on-Avon
•START / FINISH•	Grid reference: ST 824606 (on Explorer 156)
•DOG FRIENDLINESS•	On lead through town
•PARKING•	Bradford-on-Avon Station car park (charge)
•PUBLIC TOILETS•	Station car park

BACKGROUND TO THE WALK

Set in the wooded Avon Valley, Bradford is one of Wiltshire's loveliest towns, combining historical charm, appealing architecture and dramatic topography. It is often likened to a miniature Bath, the town sharing the same honey-coloured limestone and the elegant terraces and steep winding streets that rise sharply away from the river. Historically a 'broad ford' across the Avon, the original Iron-Age settlement was expanded in turn by the Romans and Saxons, the latter giving Bradford its greatest treasure, St Laurence's Church. The Avon was spanned by a fine stone bridge in the 13th century – two of its arches survive in the present 17th-century structure – and by the 1630s Bradford had grown into a powerful centre for the cloth and woollen industries.

Wealthy Wool Town

You will find exploring the riverside and the lanes, alleys and flights of steps up the north slope of the town most rewarding. Beautiful terraces are lined with elegant 18th-century merchants' houses with walled gardens, and charming 17th- and 18th-century weavers' cottages, the best examples being located along Newtown, Middle Rank and Tory terraces. The latter is the highest and affords superb views of the town. The wealth needed to make all this building possible came from the manufacture of woollen cloth. In the early 1700s Daniel Defoe, author of *Robinson Crusoe*, commented 'They told me at Bradford that it was no extra-ordinary thing to have clothiers in that county worth from £10,000 to £40,000 per man'. Bradford's prosperity at the time is reflected in the size of the magnificent 14th-century tithe barn at Barton Farm.

With the development of mechanisation, the wool trade moved from individual houses to large water and steam driven mills alongside the Avon. At the time the Kennet and Avon Canal was built, in 1810, the town supported around 30 mills and some of these buildings survive, in various degrees of restoration or disrepair, today. With the centre of the wool trade shifting to Yorkshire, the industry declined during the 19th century and the last of the mills closed in 1905. The town is now prosperous once again with tourists and new residents, many of them commuting to Bath, Bristol and even London.

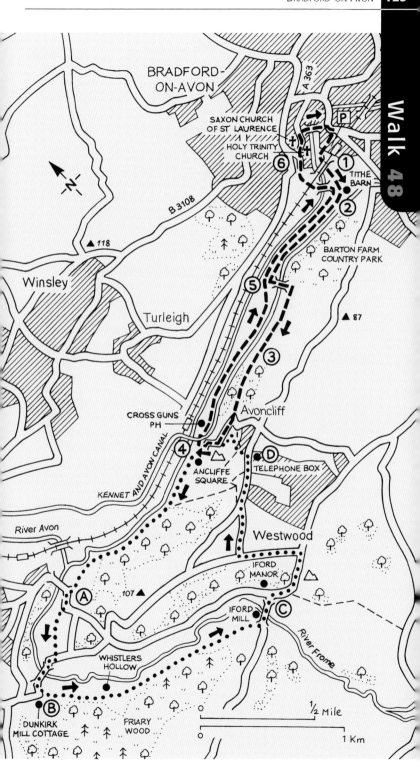

BRADFORD-
ON-AVON

A 363

SAXON CHURCH
OF ST LAURENCE
HOLY TRINITY
CHURCH

⑥

P

①

TITHE
BARN

②

BARTON FARM
COUNTRY PARK

B 3108

▲ 118

Winsley

⑤

Turleigh

▲ 87

③

Avoncliff

CROSS GUNS
PH

④

ANCLIFFE
SQUARE

Ⓓ

TELEPHONE BOX

KENNET AND AVON CANAL

River Avon

Westwood

IFORD
MANOR

Ⓐ

107 ▲

IFORD
MILL

Ⓒ

River Frome

WHISTLERS
HOLLOW

Ⓑ

DUNKIRK
MILL COTTAGE

FRIARY
WOOD

½ Mile

1 Km

Walk 48

Down by the river, the tiny, bare Saxon Church of St Laurence is the jewel in Bradford's crown and you should not miss it! It was founded by St Aldhelm, the Abbot of Malmesbury, in AD 700 and this building dates from the 10th century. For centuries it was forgotten; the chancel became a house, the nave a school, and the west wall formed part of a factory. The true origins and purpose of the building were rediscovered in 1858 and it remains one of the best preserved Saxon churches in England.

Walk 48 Directions

① Walk to the end of the car park, away from the station, and follow the path left beneath the railway and beside the **River Avon**. Enter **Barton Farm Country Park** and keep to the path across a grassy area to an information board. With the packhorse bridge right, keep ahead to the right of the tithe barn to the **Kennet and Avon Canal**.

> **WHAT TO LOOK FOR** ⓘ
> Note the a small, dome-shaped building at the south end of Town Bridge. Called the 'Chapel', it was, in fact, a lock-up or 'blind house' containing two cells with iron bedsteads for prisoners.

② Turn right along the tow path. Cross the bridge over the canal in ½ mile (800m) and follow the path right to a footbridge and stile. Proceed along the right-hand field edge to a further stile, then bear diagonally left uphill away from the canal to a kissing gate.

> **WHERE TO EAT AND DRINK** ⓘ
> In Bradford-on-Avon, try the **Cottage Co-operative Café** behind the tourist information centre, the **Dandy Lion** in Market Street and the **Canal Tavern** or the **Lock Inn Canalside Café** on Frome Road. At Avoncliff, the **Cross Guns** offers traditional pub food and a splendid terraced riverside garden, while lunches and teas are served at the **Mad Hatter Tea Rooms**. On Walk 49, enjoy a pint at the **Freshford Inn**.

③ Follow the path through the edge of woodland. Keep to the path as it bears left uphill through the trees to reach a metalled lane. Turn right and walk steeply downhill to **Avoncliff** and the canal.

④ Don't cross the aqueduct, instead pass the **Mad Hatter Tea Rooms**, descend the steps on your right and pass beneath the canal. Keep right by the **Cross Guns** and join the tow path towards **Bradford-on-Avon**. Continue for ¾ mile (1.2km) to the bridge passed on your outward route.

⑤ Bear off left downhill along a metalled track and follow it beside the River Avon back into **Barton Farm Country Park**. Cross the packhorse bridge and the railway to **Barton Orchard**.

⑥ Follow the alleyway to **Church Street** and continue ahead to pass the **Holy Trinity Church** and the Saxon **Church of St Laurence**. Cross the footbridge and walk through St Margaret's car park to the road. Turn right, then right again back into the station car park.

> **WHILE YOU'RE THERE**
> Discover the natural and historical heritage of Bradford with a visit to the town's fascinating **museum**. Linger at **Barton Farm Country Park** to view the craft shops in the former medieval farm buildings, and marvel at the great beams and rafters of Bradford's magnificent, tithe barn, the second largest in Britain.

Through the Frome Valley

Extend your walk through the beautiful Frome Valley.
See map and information panel for Walk 48

•DISTANCE•	3½ miles (5.7km)
•MINIMUM TIME•	2hrs
•ASCENT / GRADIENT•	344ft (105m) ▲▲▲
•LEVEL OF DIFFICULTY•	🚶🚶🚶

Walk 49 Directions (Walk 48 option)

At **Avoncliff**, Point ④, pass the tea rooms and turn left along the track and pass the old workhouse (**Ancliffe Square**), now modern apartments. As the track veers left, keep ahead through the gate and continue through trees to a further gate. Continue beside the **River Avon** to a kissing gate and follow the woodland path to a gate and continue across the water-meadow to a gate beside the bridge over the **River Frome**, Point ④.

Turn left along the lane, climb a stile on your right and cross the field to a further stile. Maintain direction towards a derelict factory to a stile and lane. Turn right, walk beside the river and cross the bridge. Keep to the lane uphill through trees and take the bridleway left in front of **Dunkirk Mill Cottage**, Point ⑧. Bear right, then take the bridle path left opposite the entrance to a large house. Continue to a gate, keep left down to a track and turn left. Turn right (yellow arrow) opposite **Whistlers Hollow** and cross the field to a stile and gate. Keep left through the field to a stile and gate

and walk through **Friary Wood** to a gate. Turn right along the field edge for nearly ½ mile (800m) to a stile in the corner. Turn left, pass **Iford Mill** and cross the bridge to Iford, Point ©.

Iford Manor dates from around 1500 and has a classical front, added in 1730 by William Chanler, a mill owner from Bradford-on-Avon. Home to the architect and landscape gardener, Harold Peto from 1899–1933, it is famed for the romantic, award-winning Italianate gardens he created on the steep hillside behind the manor. These are characterised by steps, terraces, sculpture and magnificent views.

Bear right and follow the lane steeply uphill to a junction. Turn left along the grassy verge for ¼ mile (400m) and take the bridle path right, signed '**Upper Westwood**'. Continue to a lane and turn right through **Upper Westwood**. Take the lane left opposite the telephone box, Point ⑩. Where it curves left, take the left of two footpaths ahead and head downhill through the edge of woodland. Pass beside a gate, cross a drive and rejoin the lane walked earlier, heading steeply downhill to **Avoncliff** and the **Kennet and Avon Canal**. For the return route follow Walk 48 from Point ④.

Tow Path Trail to Bath

Discover canal architecture on the this tow path walk into Somerset.

·DISTANCE·	11 miles (17.7km)
·MINIMUM TIME·	4hrs 30min
·ASCENT / GRADIENT·	Negligible
·LEVEL OF DIFFICULTY·	
·PATHS·	Canal tow path
·LANDSCAPE·	River valley and urban area
·SUGGESTED MAP·	aqua3 OS Explorers155 Bristol & Bath;156 Chippenham & Bradford-on-Avon
·START / FINISH·	Grid reference: ST 824606 (on Explorer 156)
·DOG FRIENDLINESS·	No real problems; keep under control through Bath
·PARKING·	Bradford-on-Avon Station car park
·PUBLIC TOILETS·	Bath Spa Station and car park

Walk 50 Directions

Bradford-on-Avon lies on the Kennet and Avon Canal, which stretches 87 miles (140km) from the River Avon at Bristol to the River Thames at Reading. Now fully restored, the canal offers some of the best-loved walking in Wiltshire. Between Bradford and Bath it passes through steep, wooded hillsides that rise 400ft (122m) above the Avon Valley, arguably the finest natural landscape along the length of the canal. But there is far more than just great scenery for you to savour on this memorable 11 mile (17.7km) ramble to Bath. You will discover some exceptional canal architecture, notably restored

> **WHAT TO LOOK FOR** ⓘ
> Note the **tow rope marks** etched into the tight corner of Avoncliff aqueduct and the two mills below beside the River Avon. Look for the ¼ mile (400m) **posts** showing the distance from the River Thames at Reading, and the **cast iron crane** at Dundas Wharf.

wharves, magnificent aqueducts, a 19th-century pumping station and ornately decorated tunnels.

At Bradford-on-Avon the canal company built two wharves, one below and one above the town's lock. A lock was required to raise the level of the canal to that of the Wilts and Berks Canal at Semington. On the upper wharf a stone and timber structure was built and alongside it remains the original dry dock, now in use again.

Walk to the end of the car park away from the station and follow the path left beneath the railway and beside the river. Enter **Barton Farm Country Park** and keep to the path across a grassy area to an information board. Keep ahead and pass to the left of the tithe barn to reach the **Kennet and Avon Canal**. Turn right along the tow path for 1¼ miles (2.8km) to **Avoncliff**.

With great skill, the engineer John Rennie took the canal along the winding Avon Valley crossing the

Walk 50

river twice via substantial aqueducts. Avoncliff aqueduct was built in 1804 to take the canal across the valley to the north side. It is 110yds (100m) long and features three arches, a solid parapet and balustraded ends. The Bath stone has not weathered well and has suffered from casual repair work and patching in brick.

Bear left at the **Cross Guns** and pass beneath the canal. Ascend steps and join the tow path on the opposite side. Proceed for 3 miles (4.8km) to reach the **Dundas Aqueduct**.

Perhaps the most impressive of the masonry structures on the canal, Dundas Aqueduct stands as a fitting memorial to the architectural and engineering skill of John Rennie. Built in 1804, this fine classical stone aqueduct carries the canal 64ft (19.5m) above the River Avon on a graceful wide arch spanning 65ft (19.8m), which is framed by paired giant pilasters. It is worth walking down into the valley below to really appreciate this structure. Brassknocker Basin marks the junction of the Kennet and Avon Canal with the Somerset Coal Canal, opened in 1801 to run 10 miles (16.1km) to the mines at Paulton and Radstock. It was taken over by a railway company and closed in 1898. The first ¼ mile (400m) was restored between 1986–88 for moorings.

Cross the bridge over the canal and continue for 1¼m (2km) to **Claverton Pumping Station**.

The waterwheel powered pumping station was built at Claverton in 1810 to raise the water from the Avon to the canal and is the only one of its kind on British canals. Now fully restored it is open to the public on certain days.

Keep to the tow path through the now very rural Avon Valley, with all eras of transport modes in sight – river, canal, railway and road. Beyond Bathampton, the tow path leads you through the attractive suburbs of Bath, probably the least stressful and least busy route into the heart of the city. Pass through **Sydney Gardens**, cross the canal in front of **Sydney House** and continue on the opposite side of the canal. At the bottom of **Bathwick Hill**, cross the road and canal and continue along the tow path, passing locks to reach the **A36**.

Cross the lock gates on your left, drop down steps and pass beneath the road. Soon you'll reach the junction where the canal meets the River Avon. Do not follow the riverside path ahead, instead bear left along the pavement and turn right across the footbridge over the Avon to reach **Bath Spa Station**. Return to **Bradford-on-Avon** via the hourly train service (every 2 hours on Sunday).

Walking in Safety

All these walks are suitable for any reasonably fit person, but less experienced walkers should try the easier walks first. Route finding is usually straightforward, but you will find that an Ordnance Survey map is a useful addition to the route maps and descriptions.

Risks

Although each walk here has been researched with a view to minimising the risks to the walkers who follow its route, no walk in the countryside can be considered to be completely free from risk. Walking in the outdoors will always require a degree of common sense and judgement to ensure that it is as safe as possible.

- Be particularly careful on cliff paths and in upland terrain, where the consequences of a slip can be very serious.

- Remember to check tidal conditions before walking on the seashore.

- Some sections of route are by, or cross, busy roads. Take care and remember traffic is a danger even on minor country lanes.

- Be careful around farmyard machinery and livestock, especially if you have children with you.

- Be aware of the consequences of changes in the weather and check the forecast before you set out. Carry spare clothing and a torch if you are walking in the winter months. Remember the weather can change very quickly at any time of the year, and in moorland and heathland areas, mist and fog can make route finding much harder. Don't set out in these conditions unless you are confident of your navigation skills in poor visibility. In summer remember to take account of the heat and sun; wear a hat and carry spare water.

- On walks away from centres of population you should carry a whistle and survival bag. If you do have an accident requiring the emergency services, make a note of your position as accurately as possible and dial 999.

Acknowledgements

The author would like to thank Bonita Toms, Peter Toms and Lucy Piper, who assisted in check-walking some of the routes, and the staff at Bradford-on-Avon, Devizes, Malmesbury, Marlborough and Salisbury tourist information centres for their invaluable assistance.

AA Publishing and Outcrop Publishing Services would like to thank Chartech for supplying aqua3 maps for this book. For more information visit their website: www.aqua3.com.

Series management: Outcrop Publishing Services Ltd, Cumbria
Series editor: Chris Bagshaw
Front cover: AA Photo Library/E Meacher